JANE WITHERS   PHOTOGRAPHS BY **CHRISTOPH KICHERER**

HOT water

bathing and the contemporary bathroom

QUADRILLE

CONTENTS

ATTITUDES TO BATHING

Throughout history, attitudes to bathing have changed from epoch to epoch and society to society, influenced by religious and cultural views on hygiene and health, as well as on the body and sexuality. As deeply rooted in our sense of identity as food or sex, Brillat Savarin's observation 'Tell me what you eat and I'll tell you who you are' could just as easily be applied to how we wash.

While the court at Versailles under Louis XV enjoyed more sophisticated bathing habits (if not sanitation) than is often supposed, and had at least 100 bathrooms – including a monumental rose-marble octagonal bath built for the Sun King – it was not until 1851 that the first bathtub was installed in the American White House. Although the Japanese of all classes in the Edo period frequented communal bath houses, most city dwellers in Paris or London at the same time had to make do with the washstand or courtyard tap. Where the Roman baths were hydro-pleasure-domes incorporating exercise grounds and debating chambers, food and sex, Islam transformed this institution into the poetic tranquillity of the hamam. If the Christian moral backlash spelled the final end for the hedonistic bathing culture of antiquity, the church was also responsible for closing down the 'stews' of medieval London and making public bath houses extinct in much of Europe. But, while sixteenth-century Spain was in the dark ages of sanitation, Spaniards arriving in the Americas found Mayan tribes and Aztecs enjoying elaborate bathing rituals in 'temescal' sweat houses.

For much of the twentieth century, at least in the west, bathing has been constrained by the hangover of Victorian prudery and the early modern cult of physical and mental hygiene at the expense of sensuality and pleasure. While there have always been exceptional private bathrooms, generally bathing has been reduced to little more than a hygienic duty and the bathroom a closeted space more attuned to clinical correctness than pleasure.

Even with the arrival of running hot and cold water, attitudes were slow to change. The influential book *The Bathroom* published in 1974, an analysis of the ergonomics of bathing with diagrams illustrating

such strange phenomena as 'the dispersion of the male urine stream' and 'typical movements involved in entering and leaving a conventional tub', reduced bathing to a mechanical process to be incorporated with maximum efficiency in the minimum space.

Yet now what was once considered a 'forbidden' space is taking on a new importance, and being integrated into the home in unexpected ways. This has very little to do with technological progress – it is curious just how little the bathroom has evolved during the last century compared with other areas of the house – and much more to do with how we use and prioritize domestic space, and the importance we attach to the ritual of bathing.

As well as a physical space, the bathroom has an intense psychological dimension, and carries an emotional and erotic charge. It may be the only place in which we have time to relax, reflect, confront ourselves naked in the mirror or indulge in sybaritic rituals. Given the time we spend in the bathroom, why shouldn't it be enjoyable? It has been estimated that the average person spends 23 years of their lifetime sleeping, four and a half years eating and two years in the bath, although I suspect that for keen bathers one could multiply this at least four or five times. In our increasingly open living spaces where there is little allowance for privacy, the bathroom may be our only legitimate sanctuary.

ABOVE *The monumental washbasin in the Caldarium at the Forum Baths, Pompeii.*

The current resurrection of the bathroom is part of larger shifts in domestic space. If the kitchen has been transformed in the post-war era from a necessary adjunct to domestic life into the heart of more sociable, open living spaces, the bathroom is going through a similar reinvention. And if the kitchen's reinvention has much to with the symbolic importance of nourishment in the home, the bathroom equally is associated with physical rejuvenation and sensory pleasures.

It also reflects changing attitudes to sexuality. If the closeted bathroom in the traditional bourgeois home is seen as representing – or reinforcing – closeted sexuality, making it into a more sociable or explicitly eroticized space is a deliberate reaction against the veil conventionally thrown over rooms associated with sexuality in the home. Bathing enthusiasts, designers and architects are deliberately playing with these boundaries: in one Australian house the tub has been repositioned on the front porch (see pages 118-19).

LEFT *A basin carved in limestone by John Pawson.*

ABOVE *In a New York loft the utilitarian approach is in keeping with the industrial building.*

Like the kitchen, the bathroom has been widely accepted as a domestic status symbol, a currency of fantasy lifestyles and often a mecca for lavish bad taste. A Californian architect whose trademark bathrooms are acerbic visual puns told me that, along with the kitchen, the bathroom was the place on which clients were willing to spend most money because they felt they had something to show for it. But if the age of the avocado suite is over, the trend for architects and designers to make the bathroom the hallmark of their domestic work with expensive custom-made fittings often seems to lack sensitivity and sensuality, the understanding of surface and texture that is fundamental to bathing.

The resurrection of the bathroom is part of a much broader interest in health, and in regaining a physical and spiritual balance in our lives. As Siegfried Giedion, architectural historian, observed, 'The role that bathing plays within a culture reveals the culture's attitude toward human relaxation. It is a measure of how far individual well-being is regarded as an indispensable part of community life.' A holistic approach to bathing as a process of physical and spiritual renewal, balancing relaxation and rejuvenation, the cleansing of the body and the symbolic purification of the mind or soul is deeply rooted in many cultures. In our quest to enrich the bathing experience we are beginning to explore this lost dimension.

This desire for ritual and sensuality is reflected in the growth in hydrotherapy and spas, and the mass consumption of bathroom lotions and potions. Yet it is ironic that as we dismantle the rituals that once framed our own lives, we desperately adopt customs from other cultures, whether seaweed wraps, hot tubs or ass's milk baths. Californian climate and lifestyle have done much to promote a hedonistic bathing culture symbolized by the pool and hot tub and popularized through the movies, where bathing provided an excuse for nudity and seduction just as it did for orientalist artists. The archetypal Californian dream home is brilliantly parodied in Peter Sellers, *The Party* where the whole house becomes a giant bubble bath.

But the million-gallon question is, what makes a great or even pleasurable bathroom? Certainly, it is not simply about the space or the fittings, or baths with consoles attached that look as though they could drive a spacecraft, let alone the ergonomic efficiency of the sanitary engineers. This is a complex room to plan, and because of the fixed services perhaps the most immutable in the home. Although efficient

RIGHT *The sculptural form of the* chaise-longue *defines the bathroom in Le Corbusier's Villa Savoye.*

plumbing is a prerequisite, neither state-of-the-art wealth nor technological supremacy are any guarantee of an agreeable bathing environment. In fact, very often the opposite is true. 'In the end, the bath requires very little: essentially it needs a new attitude in the way we use it . . . ', observes designer Piero Lissoni. 'We need to rediscover the cultural dimension of the bath, well-being as a simple, natural human need.'

Some of the most memorable bathing experiences take place way outside the confines of the conventional bathroom, recalling the days before water was piped to man, and man had to go to water if he wanted a bath. Leonard Koren's passionate bathing manifesto *Undesigning the Bath* is a paean to great bathing experiences, celebrating the earthy and animistic over more recent attempts to domesticate the bathroom. Koren's sublime baths include natural hot springs and thermal waterfalls that pound the body like massage jets, as well as the hamam and the Apache Indian sweat lodge, an igloo-shaped portable sauna made from a wooden frame covered in skins.

ABOVE *The house becomes a giant bubble bath in Peter Sellers' film* The Party.

Deeply rooted within such experiences is contact with nature and the elements, and cultural memories of water. Water is celebrated as a powerful metaphysical as well as physical life force in the religious rites and creation myths of all ancient and primitive cultures, and in certain societies this is kept alive today. Although Japanese or Scandinavian bathrooms keep pace with modern technology, they are also deeply rooted in a tradition that celebrates an intense relationship with water in a way that tends to be negated in western life. As designer Andrée Putman observes, 'It is strange that water, which is so naturally untrammelled and limitless, should be so curbed and channelled, as if neutralized in the town . . .' With increasing ecological awareness, we are beginning to regain something of this respect for water and the earth's limited natural resources. Yet there is also something deeply contrary about a world where we build bathrooms as if water supplies were limitless and then pay dearly for purity in bottled form.

Bathing *aficionados* and certain architects and designers are exploring antiquity and non-western traditions to rediscover a more celebratory view of bathing and a cultural and sensual dimension lost to the west. Lissoni characterizes 'the design and the architecture of the bath as a place of elegant simplicity.

LEFT *The hot tub on the deck of John Lautner's Sheats residence overlooks Los Angeles.*

ABOVE *A hot shower on the terrace of architectural designer Charles Rutherfoord's London house.*

A simplicity which is connected with the natural act of washing and, in different ways, is manifest in the culture of all civilization.' In fact, many of today's more sympathetic bathing environments have more in common with the communal foot-washing bath at the Inn at Knossos on Crete, a room of rigorous austerity built entirely of stone with a deep pool sunk in the centre, than the lavish bathroom in the Minoan Queen's apartments.

But although there is a lot that we can learn from other cultures, it has little to do with direct emulation and more with the sensibility behind it. And even when we do adopt the bathing rituals of other societies, we tend to put our own cultural spin on them. The celebrated nineteenth-century spas may have been intended to emulate the splendour of Roman baths, but the emphasis was redirected towards medicinal cures and the atmosphere of a sanitorium. Similarly, the rectangular wooden soak tub of Japanese origin has become associated in the west with minimalist interiors.

Many of the most successful contemporary bathing environments absorb elements of other traditions without resorting to literal references or pastiche. This can manifest in the value placed on sculptural simplicity; the use of natural materials, such as the feel of a wooden tub or stone underfoot; the subtlety of muted light, as in the hamam; the cocooning warmth of steam; and not least the pure enjoyment of bathing and the movement of water. In Peter Zumthor's spa at Vals in Switzerland, the austere grandeur of rock and water is evocative of many ancient bathing places, while certain minimalist bathrooms encapsulate the essential austerity of Japanese bath-house design in sculptural modern form. Although there are many venerable bathing traditions still alive today – not least the Russian *bania* or the spas of Budapest – I have focused on three that have particular contemporary resonance, whether on an aesthetic or formal level, or through ritual and sensuality, and these are described in the next section.

Koren argues vehemently that no contemporary architect or designer is capable of designing a great bathroom, and that their concern with hardware and technical virtuosity is 'a minor virtue considering the total constellation of elements that constitute a great bath', yet I hope that some of the bathrooms here show this is beginning to change.

RIGHT *Richard Leplastrier sites an open-air bathroom on a deck overlooking water.*

BATHING TRADITIONS

The Hamam

The Roman passion for bathing and building great bath houses laid down the roots of a bathing culture that flourished around the Mediterranean and across Europe long after the empire fell. The remnants can still be seen from Carthage to Baden Baden or Bath, but the most direct descendant of the Roman *thermae* is the hamam or Turkish bath, still in use throughout much of the Islamic world and an extraordinary survivor of a world cocooned in sensuality.

Although the hamam is modelled on the baths of antiquity, historians note how the Arabs adapted the Roman institution to their own needs. Whereas the Romans, baths were a hub of social and political life, the interior world of the hamam reflects the quiet and repose of Muslim culture. Athletic activity and debate were replaced by massage, music, contemplation and, of course, gossip. While the Roman baths were flooded with daylight, the hamam is a muted world of steam and shadows, pierced by shafts of sunlight. The Romans also supported mixed bathing until things got out of hand, but in Muslim culture bathing is strictly segregated and complies with Islamic laws of hygiene and ritual purification.

Istanbul, where the Turks built on Byzantine tradition, is the world's hamam capital. At its height, every district had a communal hamam, initially for men, and only later opened for women at certain times, but now many have closed down or sunk into terminal dilapidation. In *Hamam the Turkish Bath* director Ferzan Ozpetek captures the seductive languor and latent eroticism of this fading institution. Part of the thrill is the sense of mystery. From the street there is little clue – other than the dome studded with glass to illuminate the great hall beneath – as to what goes on inside these marble palaces. Inside, insulated from the cacophony of the street, although plastic buckets and old tins have replaced silver bowls, garish sarongs the rich Ottoman textiles, and flip-flops the wooden hamam clogs as tall as platforms, the magic survives.

ABOVE *The entrance to the Kachachine hamam in Tunis.*

LEFT *The domed hot room.*

In the baths of Istanbul, the Ottoman Turks adopted a cruciform plan, with the great domed hot room at the heart of the establishment. Like the Roman prototypes, the hamam is heated by an underfloor hypercaust system, so the marble is warm underfoot. Beneath the great dome is a marble podium, usually polygonal in shape, draped with bodies or used for massage. Details such as the way channels are cut in the marble to ensure dirty water runs away reveal the knowledge and skill involved in traditional hamam design. The muted quality of lighting is essential, and small skylights are shaped and positioned to create rays of light cutting through the steamy chiaroscuro at different times of day. Occasionally you still find oil lamps in use at night, but all too often fluorescent tubes kill the ghostly atmosphere that is so much a part of this penumbral world. The grand austerity of the halls was conceived as a backdrop, animated by textiles, carpets and the pageant of hamam life, where bathers dealt in gossip with the dexterity of market traders.

The leisurely ritual of the hamam has hardly changed. First the body relaxes in steam, slowly subsumed in lassitude. After this you are scrubbed by the hamam attendant using a rough glove, and then massaged. In certain regions different earths are used to cleanse and soften the skin. In the women's hamam, a sugar mixture is used for hair removal, henna to colour the hair, and geranium and rose water for cleansing the skin. An essential part of the process is resting in the chamber of repose and drinking tea while the body comes slowly back to its senses.

The western fascination with the hamam has a long tradition among orientalist artists and writers often fixated by exoticism and licentiousness. The fashion for Turkish baths exploded in the eighteenth and nineteenth centuries, leading to the building of public and private baths outside Islam. In London, Porchester Baths (among others) survive from this era. In Paris, the hispano-Moorish hamam attached to the mosque built in the 1920s is still in use today.

Although superficially the culture of the hamam may seem to have little obvious connection to the domestic bathroom, the aesthetic and sensibility, the dramatic manipulation of light and the treatment of stone, as well as the ritual of grooming and the deep sensuality of relaxation, are profoundly relevant to the modern bathing experience.

Japanese Bathing

There are few people who take as much pleasure in bathing as the Japanese, and few societies that have developed such a sophisticated bathing culture. Given the kaleidoscopic pace at which Japanese culture consumes trends, it seems remarkable that bathing rituals have remained so deeply ingrained. 'Ultimately to be in Japan is to enter the *furo* [bath] again – to shed one's workday clothes, bathe leisurely and don a comfortable household *yukata* before dinner,' wrote the sculptor Isamu Noguchi, '. . . It is the *furo* and the *o-yu* [hot water] that help us remember, even in our cramped little modern tubs, submerged to our necks in water, we luxuriate in our memories of time and space, and feel ourselves alive once again.'

Much more than a hygienic necessity, in Japan bathing is as much a process of spiritual rejuvenation as physical relaxation, justifying the truism that 'Americans bathe to get clean, Japanese clean to bathe.' Washing is a separate operation which takes place first outside the tub – the tub itself is a place for repose and reflection where the aroma of the wood, the temperature of the water, the steam and the depth of the tub all contribute to inducing deep quietude.

This profound belief in the ritual of purification is deeply rooted in the Shinto ethos, where cleanliness is a central tenet in the same way that simplicity and purity are fundamental to the aesthetic. It is reflected in the serenity and the refinement of details of traditional bath-house design. In a modest rustic inn such as the Azumaya, the bath house stands slightly apart, a tall room clad in dark wood melting in a fug of mildly sulphurous steam from the hot spring waters. The soft wooden floor is subtly sloped so that the soapy washing water drains away from the tub;

BELOW *The communal wooden bath in the public bath house at the hot spring resort of Yunomine.*

the grid of the window is reflected in the black water mirror. The large communal bath is made from *hinoki* cypress wood worn so soft it flakes into the water. The simplicity, even austerity, of the design is intended to free the mind from distractions and induce a state of meditative calm – as the body floats, the mind wanders.

The Japanese call those addicted to bathing 'ofuroholics', and the state that one hopes to attain is called *yudedako*, a level of contentment which translates literally as 'boiled octopus', referring to the colour bathers turn after soaking in waters which by western standards can be almost unbearably hot.

Although in the domestic bathroom a cramped acrylic or

enamel tub has pretty much taken over from the traditional wooden tub, the social aspect of communal bathing remains important. Traditional bathing rituals still flourish at *onsen* hot spring resorts, where families and groups of friends gather much as westerners flock to the seaside, and bathing is a massive tourist industry.

This reverence for water is nurtured by Japan's rich resources. There are estimated to be at least twenty thousand hot springs erupting, bubbling and spraying from the volcanic islands. Each spring water has different properties and benefits: while some are rich in minerals, others are scented by hibiscus or pine. They are located everywhere, from high mountain springs where you can bathe in rock pools, to the seaside where warm water spurts into underwater caves, or thermal waterfalls.

A passion for novelty affects bathing as much as other areas of Japanese life. In the Edo period, bath houses were built on boats and bathers soaked in tubs suspended in the water like hammocks and swayed by the motion of the river. A modern version of this is the cable car converted into a flying bathtub, whisking bathers over a craggy coastline. Popular *onsen* villages and towns have grown into concrete techno jungles with kitsch bathing palaces where you can play at Cleopatra or bathe in pools surrounded by statues of Venus where water cascades from *sake* bottles. Nevertheless, more remote spas still offer a route to an old Japan largely westernized out of urban existence.

ABOVE *The outdoor stone rotenburo.*

The experience of nature is an important part of bathing and most spas have some sort of *rotenburo* outdoor bath where you can soak sociably under the stars. These are the precursors to the Californian hot tub, but as Akiko Busch observes in *Geography of Home*, 'In trying to adopt the customs of the Japanese hot tub, for example, we have managed to transform it from a soothing family ritual to a place for romantic exchange – with all the innate tensions that invariably attend such gatherings.'

In the west, the Japanese wooden soak tub has become something of a status symbol adopted in minimalist-style bathrooms. But the relevance of Japanese bathing culture outside Japan has less to do with style or literal details – indeed, there is something faintly ridiculous about a copy of a Japanese bath house in the west – than with what we can learn from the sensibility behind it, the intense relationship with water, the use of natural materials and the value placed on simplicity, austerity and absolute visual calm.

FOLLOWING PAGES *The bath house of the Azumaya inn in Yunomine*

Sauna

While many early cultures had some form of sweat bath, the Finns have made the sauna a national tradition and popularized it all around the world. In Finland there are none of the red-light district connotations associated with the sauna elsewhere, and the almost reverential attitude to it has helped prevent the corruption that eventually brought about the demise of most other communal bathing institutions in Europe. Traditionally, the sauna was not just a place to get clean, the warm hygienic room also served as a social centre and ad hoc hospital.

Traditional sauna buildings are made from split logs, preferably mellowed with age, and sometimes with turf roofs, reflecting the Finns' attachment to rustic simplicity. Ideally they are sited by water, and the contrast of extreme temperatures – whether jumping into cold Nordic waters or rolling in snow – is part of the experience. In the rigorously unadorned interiors, wood inspires warmth and calm and is untreated so that varnish does not contaminate the steam. Lighting is kept dim to preserve the atmosphere and windows are orientated according to the paths of the sun and moon.

ABOVE *The sauna interior is built entirely in wood darkened by steam and smoke.*

Different types of sauna are characterized by the stove or *khios*. While the electric stove is adopted for urban convenience, the aroma and quality of steam from a wood fire is much preferred and purists favour the smoke sauna, where smoke is kept in the room until just before use, reducing the bathers to kippers. Proper utensils are part of the experience. The bucket and ladle used to throw water on to the hot rocks are traditionally made of wood, and towels and mats from linen. *Vihta*, the whisks used to beat the body to stimulate sweat and circulation, are dried branches of birch, linden or cedar; brushes or loofahs are used for scrubbing. Herbs such as rosemary are sometimes added to the water to scent the air.

Like most other sweat baths, the sauna has been credited with curing just about every physical and mental ailment, and although this may be exaggerated, there are certainly physiological benefits – the sauna is a swift detoxifier, helping to refresh and soften the skin.

Yet just as importantly it recalls elemental bathing experiences, and an immersion in the natural world in a way that has been drained from modern existence.

LEFT *Rural sauna buildings are traditionally sited by water.*

DEVELOPMENT OF THE MODERN BATHROOM

Although there have been private bathrooms or the possibility of such facilities in the homes of the wealthy at least since the Minoans set up palace on Crete, the real development of the modern bathroom belongs to the last two centuries and the advent of the pressurized central water supply, bringing piped water to the masses. Yet despite its attempts to appear streamlined and functional, the evolution of the modern bathroom is not so much about the development of new domestic technologies as prevailing cultural attitudes to bathing.

According to Mark Girouard in *The Victorian Country House*, by '1730 any country house could in theory have running water on all floors or as many water closets and baths as its owner wanted or could afford. But comparatively little use was made of this technology in the next 50 years.' Girouard attributes this to the conservatism of the aristocracy, who saw no need to change their habit of having a portable tub brought to the bedroom by servants and placed in front of the fire. Bathrooms such as the skylit plunge pool with piped hot and cold water designed by Sir John Soane at Wimpole Hall, Cambridgeshire, probably in 1792 when a new water system was installed, were novelties even among those with the means to achieve them. Designs as gracefully austere as Soane's or the marble tub at the Villa Kerilos are more in tune with today's aesthetic than many of their more florid or laboriously neo-classical Victorian counterparts.

The peremptoriness with which bathing was widely treated reflects deeply ingrained cultural attitudes. While early bathrooms were usually fitted in dressing rooms or bedrooms idiosyncratically converted for the purpose, devoting extensive space to what was seen as a necessary duty rather than a pleasure was considered a waste. In *Clean and Decent*, Lawrence

LEFT *The plunge bath at Wimpole Hall designed by Sir John Soane.*

ABOVE *The marble bath in the Villa Kerilos.*

Wright observes that the bathroom is 'no more thought of as a place fit for display than the scullery'. By the mid-nineteenth century the bathroom had already begun its shrinkage from a great furnished room to a compact cell – in George Vanderbilt's New York bathroom of 1855, porcelain bath, washbasin and lavatory are fairly crammed together along one wall.

Yet conservatism in the face of new technology was not confined to the aristocracy. In *Home: A Short History of an Idea*, Witold Rybczynski observes that, 'The modern bathroom with its engineered plumbing fixtures and tiled walls looked efficient and functional, but it evolved as a result of the servantless house not of any great technological advance.'

Much of the bathroom's development has been driven by the desire to reduce it to the smallest possible dimensions. By the turn of the century, in new houses in the United States the so-called 'American bathroom', a compact three-fixture room not so different from the average bathroom today, was commonplace and an important innovation in planning a small house.

An example of how simple a bathroom can be without reducing it to cold mechanics is elegantly illustrated in the double house Rudolph Schindler designed for the Schindlers and Chases in Los Angeles in 1921–22. Although extremely modest in scale and materials, the bathrooms transcend size. The built-in fittings are reduced to a minimum: a deep tub of Japanese proportions and an adjacent sink counter. Both are serviced by what Schindler called a 'plumbing tree', a skeletal arrangement of freestanding nickel-plated pipes supplying water to the bath and overhead shower on one side and basin on the other. Besides the elegant austerity, what lifts them out of the ordinary is the flood of natural light from the roof.

The need to accommodate wash facilities on ships and trains spurred on the miniaturization of the bathroom. The most extreme early domestic example of this was the prefabricated bathroom unit designed by the visionary Buckminster Fuller, who turned to the aviation and shipbuilding industries to develop his futuristic modular concepts for cheap mass housing. In 1927 he prototyped a bathroom made as a single sculptural unit in pressed steel, a precursor to the all-in-one factory-made bathroom pods fitted in hotels and office buildings. If Le Corbusier envisaged the house as a machine for living, Buckminster Fuller reduced the bathroom to a machine for cleansing.

RIGHT *The 'plumbing tree' in the Schindler house.*

Yet despite such early innovations, even today remarkably few streamlined domestic systems exist. Unlike the kitchen industry, where one company will offer a comprehensive design service, bathrooms still tend to be pieced together from different suppliers, although this is beginning to change as manufacturers start to produce ranges of complementary sanitary and hardware.

The early Modernists' ideological reworking of the home emphasized physical and mental fitness and hygiene, yet the hangover of Victorian prudery still meant that areas of the home associated with sexuality, such as the bedroom and especially the bathroom, were generally treated with clinical functionalism – and frequently continue to be. The 'ergonomic' rationalization of bathing facilities was driven by publications such as *The Bathroom* 1974, which was highly influential at the time as a sort of Kinsey report of the bathroom.

One of the most celebrated early modern bathrooms is Le Corbusier's elegant bathing suite in the Villa Savoye (1928–31) near Paris (see pages 104–5), which continues to be a point of reference for architects and designers today and, interestingly, is one of the few iconic houses from this era where the bathroom is regularly illustrated. At the time, Le Corbusier was moving towards a more lyrical approach to form, reflected here in the sculptural shape of the tiled sunken bath and *chaise-longue* curved to a feminine body form. Equally innovative is the way bathing is integrated into the sleeping space: the bathroom is really a box, which at one end is enclosed only by a curtain so that the reclining bather can enjoy the view.

Le Corbusier's pleasure in water takes wonderfully fantastic form in the

LEFT AND CENTRE *A washing area with a basin and movable bidet can be concealed behind a mobile screen in Pierre Chareau's Maison de Verre.*

Villa Sarabhai at Ahmedabad in India, where a slide shoots directly down from the grassed roof to the pool. It was supposedly inspired by André Maurois' *Fatapoufs and Thinifers*, a favourite book of the Sarabhais' son, where the bathing contraption used by the Thinifers looks a bit like a human cannon and shoots its rod-thin occupants directly from bed to bath when the alarm goes off.

Another early modern house where the approach to integrating bathing into the home has been hugely influential is Pierre Chareau's Maison de Verre (1928) in Paris. The master bathroom is not really a room: it has five entrances, and the sculptural play of screens compartmentalizes space without really dividing it, reflecting Chareau's interest in lightness and transparency. The screens can be moved to create different configurations, so that the shower and bathtub can be used at the same time with a degree of privacy – apparently tailor made for a couple where one preferred to bathe and the other to shower.

In one child's bedroom, the screen concealing the washbasin and bidet are modern reworkings of the traditional idea of a screen to wash or dress behind, made from a delicate gauze of perforated metal. In the other child's room the tub is concealed within a bookcase unit. Since Chareau's rediscovery in the 1970s by the high-tech generation, his 'engineering' approach to design has had considerable influence, as can be seen in the John Young apartment (see pages 124–27).

If an obsession with hygiene and efficiency to the detriment of the more sensual aspects of water and bathing was one facet of the Modernists' legacy, in California the climate produced a more relaxed and hedonistic bathing culture, popularizing the hot tub and outdoor shower as well as the swimming pool. In John Lautner's futuristic Sheats residence (see pages 110–15), designed in 1963 and remodelled in 1989, water is an imaginative and refreshing presence throughout the house, from the stream at the entrance to the pool to the master suite which opens on to a terrace with a sunken jacuzzi.

In the Paul Rudolph house (1973–78) in Manhattan, the bathrooms are the apotheosis of the architect's obsession with transparency, weightlessness and playful voyeurism. Unexpected views slice through floors and walls, revealing the bathroom interiors to visitors.

RIGHT *In his Manhattan town house Paul Rudolph played with transparency and unexpected views*

As well as transparent plexiglas sinks there is a transparent jacuzzi set in an upper floor which is fully visible from below.

In the 1980s, the flamboyant facilities incorporated in a new breed of design-conscious hotels, clubs and restaurants, where the lavatories were as prominent and much publicized as the dance floor or cocktail bar, helped to give the bathroom new prominence. Philippe Starck in particular made the bathrooms an epicentre of his highly theatrical creations – in the Hong Kong nightclub Felix, men urinate against a glass wall overlooking the city; in Teatriz in Madrid, the washbasin is a giant gilded table flooded with water and more like a fountain than a sink. In hip American hotels such as Morgans, the Royalton and the Delano, Andrée Putman and Starck gave the small hotel bathroom pulling power in a way that has had considerable influence on domestic bathrooms, and helped launch their own ranges of fittings.

ABOVE *A glass wall divides the bathroom from the living area and the bath is incorporated in a long tiled counter in Andrée Putman's home.*

Evolving from the home jacuzzi popularized in the 1970s and its descendant the hydromassage tub, one recent trend is towards ever more technologically sophisticated, multi-functional and expensive bathing status symbols that sometimes look frighteningly like medical equipment, recalling the chilling complexities of Victorian and Edwardian bathing contraptions. Industrial designer Marc Sadler promotes a futuristic vision of the bathroom, in which the various fixtures will be integrated into a 'water zone' that can simulate different aquatic experiences and use electronic intelligence to control 'water and air, as well as light, sound, perfume . . . all those elements which combine to create a situation of well-being'.

Yet in the 1990s, a number of architects and designers have turned away from such technologies, as well as the ergonomically driven, soulless solutions of the hygiene engineers, looking instead to ancient cultures and more elemental experiences to revive the sensual and celebratory aspects of bathing. John Pawson, who frequently makes bathrooms a defining moment in his domestic architecture, cites wide references – from the dramatic manipulation of light in the Forum Baths in Pompeii to the essential simplicity of the Japanese bath house or the sculptural forms of Cistercian fonts. Claudio Silvestrin designs, such as the massive bowl-shaped stone bath, are also characterized by a sculptural simplicity that recalls ancient rituals in

LEFT *Freestanding fittings are positioned like furniture in Philippe Starck's bathroom.*

ABOVE *Ayse Birsel's 'water room' is conceived as a futuristic landscape.* RIGHT *The bathroom is positioned at the heart of Ushida Findlay's Soft and Hairy House.*

modern form. In Richard Leplastrier's outdoor bathrooms, constructed with almost ad hoc simplicity, nature is the defining experience.

With the increasing move away from the rigid corsetry of the cellular room plan towards more open, fluid living spaces without strict divisions between public and private zones, popularized by the loft concept of living, designers are exploring new ways of incorporating bathing and the presence of water into the home, and heightening its physical and psychological presence. In a Manhattan loft designed by Winka Dubbeldam (see pages 48–51), the bathroom is enclosed by a translucent glass screen so that the sound of water and the silhouettes of bathers are present in the main living space, explicitly eroticizing bathing and making it central to the living experience. In Ushida Findlay's organo-sci-fi Soft and Hairy House in Tokyo, the positioning of the womb-like bathroom at the centre of the home with other spaces folding out from it rather like a snail's shell reflects the importance the Japanese attach to bathing.

Ayse Birsel's lyrical concept for a 'water room' is a total water environment in which how we wash and the fixtures we require have been radically rethought, based on Birsel's study of the natural movement of water. The strangely futuristic room is conceived as an abstracted island surrounded by water, where different features are incorporated into an undulating moulded concrete floor, recreating the way water is found in nature. The bath is a smooth pool filled by a cascade of water. The squatting lavatory (for Birsel, the most natural method) is integrated into a hill with a stone to lean against. On the back wall a waterfall replaces a conventional basin for washing hands and face.

Such imaginative concepts point the way to a more sensual and celebratory approach to bathing and the presence of water that is beginning to influence the way many designers think, and is helping to restore a more humane dimension that has been largely lost to the west – at least in recent history.

FOLLOWING PAGES *The spacious bathroom is treated with rigorous simplicity in the Neuendorf House by John Pawson and Claudio Silvestrin.*

The
Contemporary
Bathroom

THE BATHING ROOM

When hotelier Ian Schrager issued a brief for renovating his New York apartment, one request that stood out was for the master bedroom suite to contain a bedroom, library and lounging area and a bathroom – call it a spa, if you like – equal in size to the other areas put together. More than just a place to wash, it was to be a room in which to relax or take a nap, even a sociable space; in other words, a sort of wet living room. Although Schrager's vision is well beyond most means, it does reflect a much more general change in attitudes.

If the key direction in the west this century has been towards confining washing to a sealed, hygienic unit generally with all the charm of a mortuary, the bathing room represents a defiant antidote. Instead of marginalizing the bathroom, it reflects the heightened importance attached to bathing and the place it takes in domestic life, transforming what was once the smallest room in the house into a much more generous, celebratory space.

Rather like the development of the kitchen over the last few decades towards a sociable space that just happens to include cooking equipment, in the bathing room the bath sometimes seems almost incidental. In *Home: A Short History of an Idea*, Witold Rybczynski notes that, 'When houses contained many more rooms, bathrooms could be small. Today, the bathroom must accommodate activities which previously took place in dressing rooms, nurseries and boudoirs (even washing machines are now located in bathrooms).'

Thus, on a practical level the bathroom may be a place where we spend a good proportion of our waking time. It may also be the one room where a couple or even a family have a chance to communicate. Equally, in our move towards increasingly open living spaces, the bathroom may be the only really intimate or private place in the home. In a London house recently converted to open-plan living, the bathroom now doubles as a dressing room and is furnished in the manner of a modern boudoir (see pages 42–47).

Yet the bathroom is also a psychological space with a different mental and emotional temperature from other rooms, a place of fantasy as well as actuality, representing a dimension of freedom for the imagination as well as the body. In a SoHo loft, the bathroom opens into the bedroom on one side and the library on the other, acknowledging that bathroom and bedroom are often the places where we read (see pages 48–51).

In some ways – though certainly not always in terms of a throwback to period style – the bathing room recalls the comfort of an era before modern plumbing confined bathing to the purpose-designed fitted bathroom. In the homes of the well-off, a portable bath would have been carried upstairs to the bedroom and placed in front of the fire, while in larger houses a room might have been devoted to bathing yet was still usually modelled on a living room. The bathroom supposedly fitted out for Napoleon in the Elysée Palace and recently restored is on the scale of a salon, with a chandelier and marble fireplace, decorated mirrors and carpet. Rather like the bathing rooms of today, such grandly appointed baths were not necessarily private but were used as a sort of intimate sitting room.

In designer Philippe Starck's country retreat (see page 34) the open first floor is devoted to bathing and sleeping, divided by a storage wall. Instead of streamlined fittings, freestanding sanitary ware is placed with the looseness of furniture, although the ease is deceptive and the almost old-fashioned-looking washbowl and rolltop tub are discreetly plumbed through the floor. A lamp, dressing table and chairs give it a domestic cosiness that recalls older, decidedly bourgeois, ideas of comfort.

The rooms featured here are tangible evidence of this desire to expand the role and presence of bathing in the home, making it a central and pleasurable part of daily life rather than something to be suffered as a necessary adjunct to the activities in more important rooms.

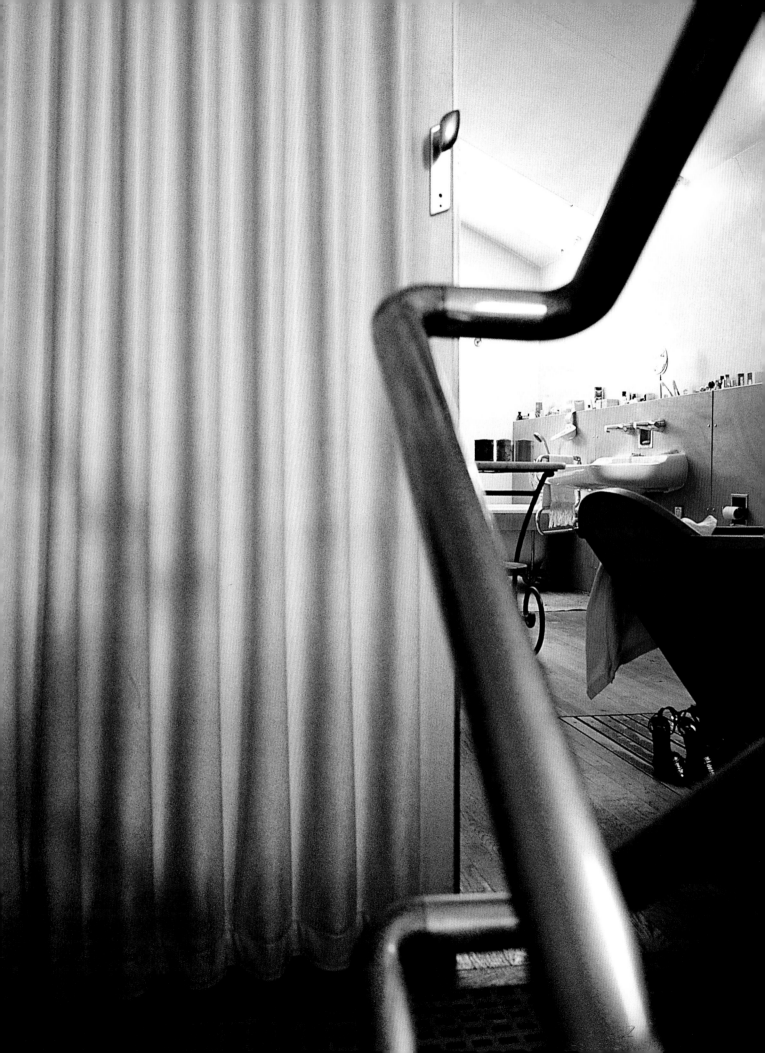

Modern Boudoir

Behind the façade of a semi-detached London house, French architect Jeff Delsalle has reconfigured the conventional cellular room plan to suit a less formal way of life than the house was designed to accommodate. In the new order, where three storeys have been morphed into two open floors linked by an industrial metal staircase, the bathroom occupies a pivotal position – easily accessible from both the living area downstairs and the sleeping quarters upstairs, and rather grandly scaled and equipped to accommodate much more than just the usual bath, basin and lavatory.

This generous allocation of space (it is directly above the kitchen and the same size) reflects the significance Swedish art director Yvonne Sporre attaches to the bathroom as a sort of private sanctuary: 'I wanted everything to be able to happen in one room, to bathe, to eat breakfast, to dress and go. It's a place to start the day. I spend too much time in the bathroom to be squashed into a small space if I have the choice.' Equally, a large multi-purpose bathroom can make sense as back-up to less structured contemporary living spaces, which require careful planning of storage and services. Here the bathroom also serves as

dressing room and laundry and a kind of private sitting room, with a substantial storage wall accommodating clothes, linen and washing machine.

If the planning is straightforward in a modern utilitarian sense, unexpected juxtapositions such as the mix of materials, textures and fittings (industrial, antique and futuristic) take the room into another stratosphere, mixing sensuality, even romance with high tech to create a modern version of the boudoir. Take the mix of baths: one is a standard acrylic model stripped of its panels to reveal the supporting clamps and moulded structure, the other an antique wooden bath.

The storage wall made from matt-varnished marine ply is balanced on one side by the low ply wall opposite, which also runs the length of the room and acts as a dock for the fittings. As well as concealing the plumbing (the wall can be removed for access), it has a sunken shelf in opaque glass for bathroom paraphernalia which is lit from beneath by waterproof marine lights. The floor is the same lime-bleached oak used throughout the house, helping to make the bathroom feel like an extension of the living space. If the bathroom is elevated from a supporting role in the home and filled with furniture that seems to have been heisted from the living room, its engagingly schizophrenic appearance reflects the fact that it is not only a hub of activity, but also a place we associate with such elusive qualities as privacy, security and comfort.

PRECEDING PAGES.
The unexpected mix of furnishings and fittings make this more like a private living room than a conventional bathroom. The bath and basin are Ideal Standard and the bath panels have been omitted to reveal the skeletal supports. The wall-hung lavatory is coupled with a concealed cistern with a press-panel flush by Geberit. The futuristic taps by Sheardown look fairly extraordinary. The folding screen door is manufactured for use in hospitals and is soundproofed.

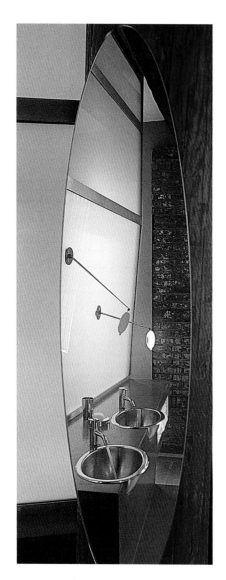

The entire bathroom is treated as a sculptural island with bath, counter and shower area built in. Constructed by specialists, the wooden form was built in sections rather like an inverted boat, lined with fibreglass, and finished with layers of intense blue plaster waxed and polished to achieve a smooth finish. The basin and bath mixers are by Vola.

Blue Island

Manhattan-based Dutch architect Winka Dubbeldam describes the bathroom in this converted SoHo loft as a 'free-floating capsule'. The idea behind the planning of the living space was to create a sense of open progression and spatial continuity, minimizing walls and doors. The bathroom is part of the master suite, open on one side to the bedroom and on the other to the library, and contained by semi-transparent glass walls which serve more as a screen than an impervious barrier, so the sounds of water are audible and the silhouettes of bathers visible in the main living space.

If the central positioning is symbolic – Dubbeldam describes the bathroom as a hinge around which space unfolds – eroticizing bathing and heightening its presence in the home, the elegant treatment of surface and texture emphasizes sensuality. 'Relaxation . . . [is] an important part of living. I think it is important to have meditative spaces in the home. When I design work spaces I make them as active as possible, but I design homes not as showcases for personalities but rather as places for them to rest.' By linking bedroom, bathroom and library, Dubbeldam creates a private zone within the openness of the apartment. The juxtaposition also acknowledges that bathroom and bedroom are intimately linked to books, as rooms where we are likely to find the calm and solitude for reading.

The bathroom itself is a deep purple-blue 'island' of intense colour within a landscape of more muted natural shades. Conceived as a single sculptural entity, with a continuous surface that folds up and down to incorporate the different elements and melds into the floor, it appears to have been carved or moulded from a solid block of blue stone, but is in fact plaster applied over a wooden form. 'Perhaps because I'm Dutch I find the pipes in New York loft buildings disturbing. Here everything is concealed, even the sprinklers are recessed into the ceiling. I wanted everything to be smooth and fluid.'

Dubbeldam plays with translucency and reflective surfaces that help to make the boundaries more ambiguous and the functions less prescriptive. The walls are custom-made glass panels, chosen to appear less dense than sandblasted glass. The blue plaster is waxed and polished to achieve a smooth, reflective, almost watery surface, and the basin and lavatory in stainless steel and the mirrors all help to dematerialize the space. The windows are concealed behind opaque glass, contrasted with a reflective metal curtain that shimmers in the light.

The sunken bathing area is treated as a room within a room, defined by the strict grid of tiles which covers stairs and bath panel as well as walls and floor.

Mexican Inquisition
Before modern concepts of privacy, the toilette was not necessarily a private but sometimes a public or at least communal affair. Here the double usage of space – salon and bathroom, stage and gallery – is reminiscent of courtly bathing ceremonies.

In the 1930s, Mexican architect Chucho Reyes, mentor to Luis Barragan, the great Mexican Modernist, reorganized the rooms behind the façade of a palazzo in Mexico City to focus inwards towards the internal courtyard and create a greater sense of privacy. The dramatically high-ceilinged bathroom is on the ground floor. Partly a cloakroom and place to bathe, partly a sort of private salon, as the rooms run directly into each other without a corridor it also serves as a private route to Chucho Reyes' apartment on the floor above.

These different functions are separated by level and treatment. While the stairs and gallery are on the same level as the adjoining rooms, the sunken bathroom gives the impression of stepping down into a pool. In contrast to the almost clinically sterile tiled washing area, the gallery is furnished more like a living room and is reminiscent of darkly theatrical baroque interiors with a piano, paintings by Chucho Reyes and his collection of chastity belts. This combined use of space playfully reverses our usual expectations, making the most private of functions potentially public.

Urban Grain

If western culture tends to value sparkling surfaces and newness over the worn, the scarred and the visibly aged, this is especially true of the bathroom, where hygiene tends to be equated with gleaming, wipeable surfaces. Yet in this loft in an industrial building in Manhattan's Flatiron district, instead of concealing the existing structure behind an overtly designed statement, the visible histories – of both the building and the objects within it – give the room much of its character.

The bathroom of around 32 sq m, which the owners describe as 'an indulgent use of space', was positioned to take advantage of an existing skylight. The entire room is panelled with tongue-and-groove boarding to above head height, lending it a utilitarian simplicity sympathetic to the sparse interior of the loft and the building's industrial past, and a sense of warmth and containment sometimes lacking in more overtly modern spaces.

The choice of old rather than new fixtures reflects the owners' preference for a 'patina of age' rather than anything too 'pristine or prissy'. In keeping with this, most of the elements are salvaged. The marble basin with taps which appear to have been caught in an arrested state of meltdown, rather like one of Salvador Dali's soft watches, was part of the original fittings from the Plaza Hotel. The pharmaceutical medicine cabinet was found on the street and rather than being spruced up has been kept in its slightly battered state. The porcelain bath dating from the 1920s is French and, like many old fittings, considerably more generous in scale than many of its modern counterparts. Although deliberately mismatched, the various elements are united by their comparatively plain design, muted colours and slightly tarnished appearance, which helps give the disparate elements a sense of unity, rather like an installation of *objets trouvés*.

Modernist Luxury

The Romans understood the sensual appeal of marble and exploited it to the full in their extravagantly embellished bathing establishments. Glacially smooth, translucent and cool to the touch, the magnetism between marble, water and flesh has transfixed architects and sculptors over many centuries. Yet more recently, marble – especially the highly polished, patterned and, more dangerously still, coloured varieties – has been derailed in the minds of many by its associations with the veneer of ersatz luxury rolled out by corporate hotel chains.

In this Manhattan penthouse, architects Marwan Al Sayed and Janet Fink have managed to evoke something of the almost decadent splendour of marble within a modernist aesthetic. Here the built-in bath is treated as a sculptural unit, and the deep surround and step make a space for sitting, or resting a book, drink or bathing utensils. But while lightweight acrylic bathtubs were developed so that the bath could be positioned more or less anywhere in the home, the weight of marble means it is only possible to install it in a fairly substantial building.

The bathroom adjoins the master bedroom, and the slit window set into the wall treated like a lightbox helps to create a more intimate sense of connection between the two rooms. The self-contained shower room is also sumptuously lined in marble and positioned to take advantage of the spectacular view grazing the Manhattan roofline. If part of the pleasure of a shower is to provide a kind of contemplative escape capsule where, insulated by the drench of water and mist of warmth, thoughts can float into another dimension, here the view is a gateway for dreams.

The luxuriously scaled bath is finished in large slabs of marble in contrasting colours, also used to line the floor, including the skirting. The shower (see following pages) is entirely lined in smaller square marble tiles laid in a chequerboard effect, including on the ceiling. The shower seat is an ochre marble shelf.

THE CELL

The self-contained bathroom – a private 'cell' where washing usually takes place behind closed doors – has become easily the most common type of wash space in the west, and one that has been almost universally adopted in industrial countries around the globe. But although the bathroom is one of the most difficult and least flexible rooms to plan and can rival the kitchen in expense, it is remarkable how little it has evolved over the last one hundred years. The compact three-fixture bathroom, commonplace in new houses in the United States by the turn of the century, is essentially the same today. Supposedly streamlined and functional, it has been endlessly worked over by sanitary engineers, yet all too often lacks in practicality as well as pleasure, justifying Andrée Putman's belief that ergonomics don't necessarily help to make a good bathroom.

How small is 'small' is a cultural issue. According to received western wisdom, the minimum space needed to dry beside a bath is 70 x 110 cm, yet in Japan, where pressure on space has forced imaginative planning, bathrooms are designed to fit in closets and baths are manufactured in a considerable range of shapes and sizes for small spaces.

Views on what the bathroom should contain also differ between cultures. In the US it is usual to have the lavatory in the bathroom, whereas in continental Europe they are generally separate. In the States it is fairly common to do away with the bath and just have a shower, and with technological advances like the power shower this is becoming more usual elsewhere. In Europe the bidet is a fairly standard fixture, but in the States it apparently still retains connotations of naughtiness and has never really caught on. In Japan, the combined lavatory, bidet and dryer is one of the few technological advances in bathroom design to have taken off. A simplified version has recently been introduced to the American market.

The chapter title 'The Cell' refers to the private nature of the space, and not necessarily the austere connotations of a monastic cell. Yet the need for practicality combined with aesthetic restraint has made sculptural simplicity one of the most enduring directions in bathroom design. The designer Piero Lissoni characterizes 'the design and architecture of the bath as a place of elegant simplicity. A simplicity which is connected with the natural act of washing and, in different ways, is manifest in the culture of all civilizations.'

The advantage of the private bathroom is that it can be a retreat, a sensory haven where an atmosphere of calm rather than activity prevails. In the bathroom designed by John Pawson (see pages 64–69), the monumental simplicity, weightiness and deep sensuality of solid, natural materials generate tranquillity. The bathroom designed by Japanese architect Masakazu Bokura (see page 72), although decidedly theatrical in appearance, plays on similar qualities, promoting an almost sanctuary-like sense of apartness. Ross Anderson's description of the small bathroom (see page 78–79) as 'sterile and beautiful and functional' is especially valid in restricted spaces where materials and detailing, and attention to issues like lighting and ventilation are particularly important.

One of the most liberating developments in the bathroom is the trend for making it a wet room, where the floor is drained so that water can spill and splash, offering a freedom in how the room is used and a celebratory enjoyment of water and its natural movement. In such environments, the claustrophobic shower cubicle is replaced by the expansiveness of an open shower. In the Pawson bathroom, the tub can be filled to the brim so that water laps over the edges. In the bathroom designed by David Hertz in Los Angeles (see pages 76–77), water cascades out of a channel cut in the side of the bath and washes over the blue stone floor, which is also an open shower area to a drainage channel. If wading across a wet floor to use the mirror can be a disadvantage, the walk-in shower partly concealed behind a wall with a drained floor is one way to create a generous shower area without turning the whole room into a pool.

Extra-sensory Perception In our

daily lives the bathroom often functions as a sort of aesthetic and neural decompression chamber, a refuge isolated and insulated from the visual and mental overload of contemporary life. If this is the case, it seems appropriate that it should adopt the sculptural simplicity of monastic imagery. In this London bathroom designed by minimalist architect John Pawson, rigorous restraint and emptiness are intended to allow space for meditation and tranquillity, a release for the senses and the mind.

Here the relatively small space is dedicated to the enjoyment of water. The massive volumes and solid, natural materials are an understated luxury, and the shadowy, cavernous darkness makes a dramatic contrast to the lightness of the rest of the house. York stone – the sandy stone of London's pavements and of the taciturn mill towns of Pawson's native Yorkshire – is used for the bath, basin, floor and benches, helping to create a sober yet at the same time sensual uniformity.

Pawson was profoundly influenced by the time he spent in Japan and has adopted some of the ritual and vocabulary of Japanese bathing. There, traditionally at least, the bathing environment is almost sacred, the various elements are reduced to a simplicity that is intended to free the mind from distractions, while the feel of natural materials and the abundance of hot water generate a deep sense of well-being. Here, in keeping with the Japanese love of communal bathing, the bathroom is a place where members of the family can splash about together. The deep rectangular soaking tub – a stone version of the

In this wet room, the floor is tanked and water drains between the paving stones. Walls are lined with a waterproof cement similar in colour to the stone. Weight is an important consideration when using large areas of stone, and may require reinforcing of the structure.

traditional wooden Japanese tub – can be filled to overflowing, with water spilling over the side on to the floor and draining down discreetly between the grid of stones. The basin is a hemisphere scooped out of a solid cube of stone and the lavatory is concealed in a bench. Such imagery also recalls the massive stone baths, basins and fonts of antique and medieval civilizations that are another continual point of reference in Pawson's work.

If Pawson's bathrooms appear dramatically austere, even ascetic to some eyes, the minimalist domestic environment is a backdrop animated by the life that goes on within it. Here the measured grid acts as a framework brought to life by the movement of bodies and water. Yet while Pawson uses natural materials that are sensual to the touch and become more beautiful with age, there is another trend to use expanses of more chilling materials such as metal in the bathroom. There is a fine line between creating a soothing atmosphere and conjuring more frightening images where nakedness is associated with vulnerability and fear.

The broadening interest in minimalism reveals shifts in the zeitgeist. Pawson recently designed an airport lounge in Hong Kong with a spa, where first-class passengers can bathe and rest in private cabanas that open on to a stream with rippling water. The choice of a minimalist architect reveals how, in certain quarters at least, ideas of luxury are shifting away from conventional padded comfort and obvious status symbols towards a refined interior world that is not about plenty but purity. Paradoxically, such restraint – the meticulous reduction to essentials – is generally costly, especially when it comes to the bathroom, where the emphasis is not on show but on concealment.

The bathroom is housed in the cylindrical core of the Glass House, a solid anchor at the heart of the transparent building. Inside, curved fittings echo the shape of the room, and the shower tray with a drain in the centre is reduced to a low tiled ridge that contains water but disappears into the floor.

Glass House

How do you deal with the bathroom in a glass house? In Mies van der Rohe's iconic Farmsworth house, the bathrooms are concealed at either end of the long wood-panelled core, which accomodates the kitchen on one side and the hearth on the other. In Philip Johnson's Miesian sibling, the consummately elegant Glass House in New Canaan, Connecticut, which the architect designed as his own residence in 1949, bathroom and chimney are housed in the enigmatic black cylinder at the heart of the domestic prism. Johnson, who once described the Glass House in snow as like 'a celestial elevator', plays on the opposition between the transparent rectilinear frame and the dark circular core, the solid and the ethereal, privacy versus openess.

Rising out of the podium and piercing through the roof, the cylinder is formally and focally the pivotal point of the house. As it contains the elements fire and water it is also the life force, a sort of giant abstract chimney.

Inside, the 3m-diameter curved room is lined with green mosaic tiles, creating an intense drench of colour within the open, transparent house that echoes the green of the neatly manicured lawn and landscape beyond. Containing lavatory, washbasin and open shower, the rounded and elliptical fittings echo the circular form of the space. At floor level the shower area is circumscribed by a circular tiled ridge that seems to disappear into the structure.

Johnson has said that the idea of the cylindrical core was inspired by 'a burnt-out wooden village I saw once where nothing was left but the foundations and chimneys of brick. Over the chimney I slipped a steel cage with a glass skin. The chimney forms the anchor.'

Monastic Calm

In this apartment in Paris, the top-floor bathroom was formerly a conservatory which architect Masakazu Bokura transformed into this deeply internalized, granite-walled room. The cell-like solemnity of the narrow, barrel-vaulted space with its diffused natural light is reminiscent of a chapel or ancient place of worship, an illusion emphasized by the tomb-like positioning of the spectacular glass bath in the centre. In Japan, says Bokura, 'the bathroom is a special place in the home, not only to wash but also to meditate and relax.'

If almost monastically austere, Bokura's handling is also decidedly theatrical, contrasting transparency and weightlessness with massiveness and solidity, so that the glass glimmers rather like shards of quartz in rock. The bath was custom-made, its form inspired by a segment of bamboo cut in half and used as a vase for flowers. The conceit of a glass bath, playing with ideas of exposure and voyeurism, still manages to be startling – even slightly disturbing – although it is an idea familiar from the aquarium. In a French engraving *A Day in the Life of a Courtesan*, a woman is climbing into a clear crystal bath designed to reveal its occupant for the delight of onlookers. In George Cukor's *The Women*, Joan Crawford as the wicked stepmother hatches Machiavellian plots from a transparent shell-shaped bath, pumped up with bubbles. In his New York town house, architect Paul Rudolph took his preoccupation with transparency and weightlessness as far as installing a cantilevered plexiglas jacuzzi visible from the living spaces below.

In order not to have even a spout detracting from the spectacular sculptural form of the glass bath, water fills from within through the waste using a custom-designed system. Panels of opaque glass conceal the windows, and the roof is also opaque creating a restful diffused light.

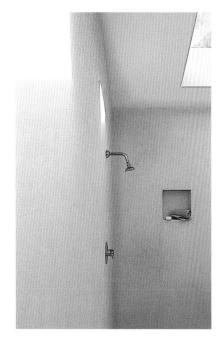 

Fairytale Logic

The unexpected collision of the rustic and the coolly modernist is characteristic of Brian Murphy, a Californian architect with a playful ability to mix visual metaphors in a way that resonates in the memory. Here the tongue-in-cheek pastoral references befit a shower room which adjoins a family games room and study in a converted stable. In fact, the idea took root pretty much by accident. When the client rejected a more straightforward design, the frustrated architect faxed him back a cartoon of this 'Hansel and Gretel' type bathing rig, and to his surprise he was given the go ahead.

But while the imagery recalls such ad hoc bathing solutions as the scene in *Seven Brides for Seven Brothers* where the brothers line up to wash a in row of wooden barrels, Murphy's detailing is far from homespun. Although it might look as though the galvanized pail just happens to be resting on the tree stump, in fact the wastepipe is plumbed through the trunk to make an effective sink. Continuing the theme, branches of silver birch serve as towel and lavatory-roll holders, and a convex traffic mirror hangs on the back of the door, throwing the room into another dimension of the surreal.

Water cascading from the bath washes over the slate floor, which doubles as a shower area and slopes to a drainage channel running along the wall. The large slate tiles emphasize scale. A boat bulkhead light is used on the shower wall.

Overflow

In the heat, an abundance of flowing water is a large part of what makes a bathroom refreshing. In this Californian bathroom, which opens on to a terrace screened by tall trees, architect David Hertz has created a space in which to splash and wallow in floods of water while feeling as if you are almost outdoors. The actual bathing area is a small, wet cell between the terrace and dressing area, with glass walls at each end and is partly glass roofed to minimize the sense of enclosure and allow for natural ventilation.

Instead of a conventional overflow, the built-in bath has a channel cut into its side rather like a sluice in a dam, so that when it fills up water floods through the gap and flows over the slightly sloping floor to a drainage channel running along the wall in the open shower area. The tub is finished in a graphite-coloured venetian plaster used for swimming pools and the same plaster is used for the walls, creating an almost cave-like feel. The floor is slate and the same stone is used for the rough ledges fixed into the walls beside the bath and the shower.

If it is not much fun having to wade across a wet floor to shave or brush your teeth here the bathing area is strictly a wet room adjoining a dry dressing area with basins and a separate lavatory, so that bathing and showering are divided off from other bathroom activities.

Shipshape

The small internal bathroom incorporating a shower over the bath, a lavatory and basin is a standard proposition, but here architect Ross Anderson shows how the ordinary can be treated with functionalist rigour and elevated through detailing and the choice of materials.

Anderson says he likes bathrooms to be 'sterile and beautiful and functional', and compares the design of this compact bathroom in a one-bedroom Manhattan apartment belonging to fashion designer Isaac Mizrahi to boat building. The analogy makes sense, given the marine industry's skill in treating wood to co-exist with water and using built-in fittings to dovetail multiple functions in a tight space. Boat building is also an industry where fitness for purpose and durability are priorities, and the levels of precision and detailing are usually considerably higher than in conventional house building.

The palette of natural but not especially luxurious materials gives the strict utilitarian design a soothing sense of warmth often lacking in more hard-edged bathrooms, where bright lighting and tiles are sometimes all too reminiscent of a laboratory or surgery. Here bath and walls are panelled in highly patterned ash, crafted to minimize exposure to water and sealed in a shiny, reflective lacquer specified for marine use. The clean, simple lines and the restraint with which the materials are treated is also reminiscent of Japanese bath-house design, as is the way formal geometric elements are played against the irregular and rough hewn – the simple rectilinear bath contrasted with the ragged pattern of the stone floor.

The basin is a contemporary version of an old-fashioned ceramic washbowl made by Waterworks. Safety codes on the use of electricity in bathrooms are necessarily strict and unusual lights may require customizing.

Theatrical Disjunction

In this guest cloakroom adjoining a shower room designed by Californian architect Brian Murphy, the chance meeting between the different worlds of the hard core and the highly decorative – the frilly swag of chandeliers strung across the ceiling as if they were fairy lights and the industrial-strength truck mirrors – sets the stage for a kind of *Easy Rider* fairytale. The tongue-in-cheek camp might be appropriate to the Hollywood location, but it is also practical, given that the mirrors are fully adjustable.

Floor, walls and ceiling are tiled in the hexagonal ceramic tiles which are very much a part of the American vernacular and are even used in restaurants in New Orleans, home town to one of the owners. Brian Murphy has made his name with a string of high-profile houses where modern design is spiked with unexpected details and a strong twist of fantasy in a way that recalls the drama of set design. In one bathroom he installed a freestanding, sandblasted glass tub fed by exposed pipes and lit theatrically from below.

Geometry

This small bathroom in the studio of artists Langlands and Bell is really a room within a room, an elliptical space constructed within a rectangular room and lit only by a skylight. The secretive, almost sepulchral mystery of this dramatically internalized room is reinforced by the central positioning of the bath, an illusion completed by a floating figure.

If the elliptical form recalls the geometry of the Enlightenment, the construction and detailing is strictly modern. Designed by architect Ashley Hicks and built by Langlands and Bell, the room is constructed using a double layer of varnished birch ply supported on a softwood frame. The voids which were left in each corner are used as alcoves housing the lavatory and washbasin (with cupboards under and over) at the far end, and cupboards at either side of the entrance which can be accessed from the anteroom.

The utilitarian character of the materials and fittings helps to ground the compact grandeur of the design. The bath taps were made by a plumber combining standard mains stopcocks with bent metal tube and are vaguely reminiscent of laboratory or industrial fittings. The lavatory, a standard ceramic model, is built into the alcove (the flush is concealed in the cupboard above). Langlands and Bell made the lavatory seat from ply and the vitreous enamel bath is similarly panelled in varnished ply, which is also used for the floor. The stainless steel sink was designed for surgical use. The alcoves are painted with varnished red emulsion, giving an effect of depth more like lacquer than ordinary gloss paint. The unity of materials and elimination of distracting details emphasize the secluded nature of the bathroom, as a private realm removed from the intrusions of everyday life.

The centrally positioned bath is supplied by hot and cold water pipes secured against the bath panel and bent to form spouts using stopcocks as taps.

Industrial Reliquary

In this downtown Manhattan loft, the low-key, almost rough-and-ready approach to the generously scaled shower room with abundant natural light is sympathetic to the urban, industrial character of the former warehouse building in TriBeCa. The previous bathroom was considerably smaller, with a false ceiling that has been removed to reveal the maze of old pipes criss-crossing the roof space, and while the walls have been panelled with tongue-and-groove wainscotting, in the upper part the raw brick – scarred by old paint and damp stains – is left exposed as a kind of visual map of the building's past.

In keeping with this, owner Stuart Parr has used salvaged elements that have a functional simplicity without appearing overtly retro. Early American fittings also tend to be larger in scale than European counterparts of a similar age. The hexagonal floor tiles, like the wainscotting, are typical of pre-war American buildings. The shower itself is a reconditioned American model from 1902; hot and cold water mix in the cylinder, so that water temperature can be controlled. The sculptural, moulded blue plastic lounger is a 1950s design, and the door is fitted with a brass ship's porthole.

The bathroom is treated as an installation within the industrial shell, a network of old and new pipes and utilitarian lighting conduit left exposed on the ceiling. The shower area is positioned at the opposite end to the basin and lavatory and has a drain in the tiled floor .

SHIFTING BOUNDARIES

Perhaps the most experimental approach to bathing today has to do with the spatial and psychological explosion of functions which were once hidden behind closed doors. By breaking down the bathroom into its component parts and repositioning the different elements, water and bathing are now being integrated into domestic life in unexpected ways. In the house Andrée Putman designed for the heroine in Peter Greenaway's film *The Pillowbook*, Putman made the vast freestanding roll-top bath pretty much the central focus of the home, a kind of eroticized love shrine set in a Zen garden, recalling a fountain or basin in formal gardens.

Although such an emphatically celebratory bathing setting might seem more probable on celluloid than in a home, increasingly relaxed attitudes to sexuality are engendering a much more open approach to bathing, drawing back the veil that was once thrown over areas of the home associated with sexuality such as the bedroom and bathroom. 'People are beginning to think about space more emotionally. The kitchen and the bathroom are rooms which are used many times in a day and can either promote sociability or the opposite – separation', observes American architect Michael Gabellini. In a Manhattan apartment, he has designed a bathroom as a glass cube which can turn from opaque to clear at the flick of a switch.

As boundaries explode, how much and what kind of privacy bathing requires becomes a personal issue defined or indeed exploited in different ways. It also depends on the nature of the household and usage – whether, for instance, a tub in a bedroom is ancillary to a more conventional bathroom. While the tub and shower have been liberated, the lavatory usually remains enclosed, although not always.

One of the more usual concepts is the merger of bathing and bedroom, a sort of elision of the bedroom suite where the walls have come tumbling down, so that bathing benefits from the scale of a proper room without absorbing the space and becomes a more sociable activity. In the Bokura project for a country house (see pages 92-97), where sleeping and bathing take place in one room, the bath can be screened by a movable storage unit, while in a small loft designed by Mark Guard (see pages 106-7), the sunken stone bath can be accessed directly from the raised bed via a swimming pool ladder, with the lavatory enclosed in a cylindrical capsule. In the open-plan De Cotiis apartment (pages 100-3), the bath is in the sleeping area, which flows unimpeded into the living quarters – not only the same space, but open to visitors as well. In the Mercer Hotel, a gentrified take on loft living designed by Christian Liaigre in Manhattan, the wall beside the bath is a folding screen which can be opened up to make the bathroom and bedroom one big room.

As with the bathing room, there are historical precedents for the current shifting of the boundaries of bathing. Before the bath or even the shower was fixed by plumbing, a portable tub might be carried to a bedroom, or in poorer households or servants' quarters simply brought into the kitchen or scullery, where water was heated up for the weekly scrub. Now, although plumbing fixes the bath or basin, it isn't necessarily in the bathroom.

One could hardly get a bolder repositioning than in the house designed by Australian architect Richard Leplastrier (see pages 116-21). Here the tub on the front porch is the first thing visitors see and the bather can enjoy a sociable soak chatting to people in the kitchen and living area. If this might seem slightly bizarre to western ideas of privacy, it could also be seen as a modern echo of the way pools or fountains were placed at the approach to a grand house and used for bathing and disporting in ways that might well surprise today's rather prissy views of heritage culture. Such defining shifts are helping to restore bathing to the heart of home life.

Modern Country

When bathing and sleeping merge in one space, the dilemma can be how to define the different areas without making the sort of impenetrable divisions that irrevocably cut up a room. In this country house outside Paris, Japanese architect Masakazu Bokura uses transparent materials and movable elements to suggest privacy without creating formal barriers, allowing the relationship of the parts to be altered at will and establishing a gentle sense of ambiguity between the two areas. Such an arrangement reflects increasingly relaxed approaches to integrating bathing into home life, balancing spontaneity and openness with intimacy and relaxation.

The bedroom on the ground floor was formerly a living room. Double doors open into the garden, recalling the way public bath houses in Japan traditionally adjoined a courtyard or garden so that bathers could enjoy the view or stroll outdoors. The sleeping area and the bath are divided by a storage unit on wheels, which is veiled in transparent plastic. It can be moved around like a screen, creating a sense of privacy without actually dividing the room, so that it would be difficult to say where sleeping ends and bathing begins. In fact, it is a sort of modern take on the old-fashioned screen which was kept in a corner and unfolded around

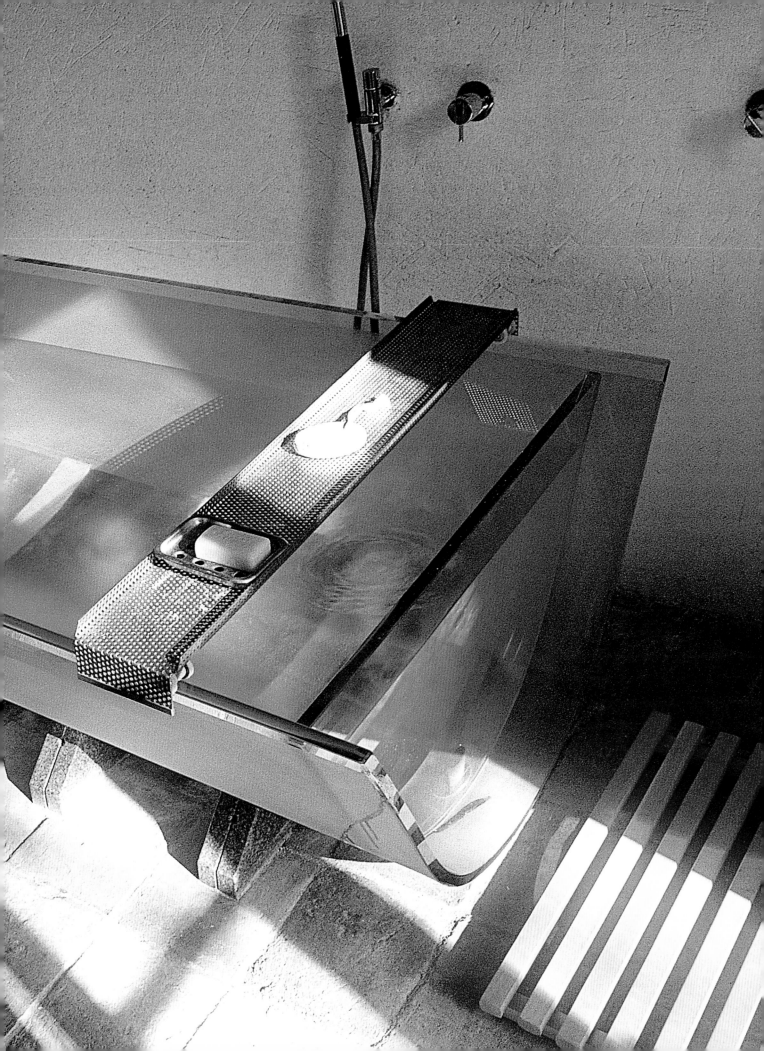

In this ground-floor bedroom and bathroom, old terracotta floor tiles and freestanding furniture designed by the architect and built in oak create a warm unity far from the cold, hard surfaces associated with the modern bathroom. The ceiling is panelled in woven willow.

a washstand for privacy, but it also houses the various utensils needed in a bathroom as well as books.

In keeping with this fluid arrangement, the bathroom fixtures are all freestanding elements, positioned much like furniture. The basin is housed in a pedestal made from the same local oak as the storage unit. The spectacular glass bathtub also plays with boundaries, hovering between the material and the ethereal, playfully revealing rather than concealing the bather. Inspired by a segment of bamboo cut in half and used as a vase for flowers, which Bokura saw in Kyoto, this technical *tour de force* was custom-made from toughened glass by French master craftsmen G. Saalburg and Desserne. To minimize the distraction of even a spout, the bath fills and empties through the base, and the mixer tap and shower are positioned to one side on the wall. The bath was originally designed by Bokura for an apartment in Paris (see page 72) but was later moved here. Set against the very traditional terracotta-tiled floor and surrounded by warm, natural materials, it could hardly appear more different than in the original granite-lined city location.

The subdued modernity, the intimate association between bathing and nature, and the use of natural materials in this country bathroom evoke the sensibility and aesthetic restraint of traditional Japanese bath-house design – a simplicity that is at once contemporary and timeless.

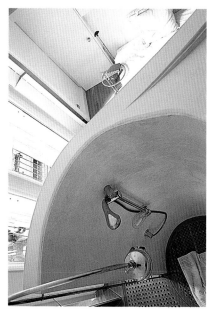

The sculptural wall concealing this small shower area is finished in travertine Armourcoat, a waterproof plaster made from marble dust. Besides the overhead shower there is second hand-held shower on an adjustable riser for washing. The pedestal basin on a stainless steel column is by Sicart. The radiator doubles as a towel heater.

Shower Capsule
How to fit a shower with a reasonable sense of privacy into a small bedroom without creating an awkward division is a fairly common design quandary. In this small flat in a house adjoining the Royal Crescent in Bath, architects Matthew and Gil Briffa overcame the problems of restricted space and the planning authority's refusal to allow alterations to the internal room plan of the listed building by installing the shower in a corner of the bedroom, screened behind a curved wall.

The sculptural form is essentially a permanent version of a folding screen in front of a washstand. Besides screening the shower, the tapering wall wraps around to conceal the separate lavatory, which is accessible from the entrance hall. According to the architects, the shape of the wall and its relation to the volume of the room were inspired by Bath's Georgian town plan, where the occasional flourish of a crescent contrasts with the rigid grid of streets. The shower floor is a custom-made teak deck raised above the level of the bedroom to accommodate a drainage tray and avoid the need for a sloping floor in such a small space.

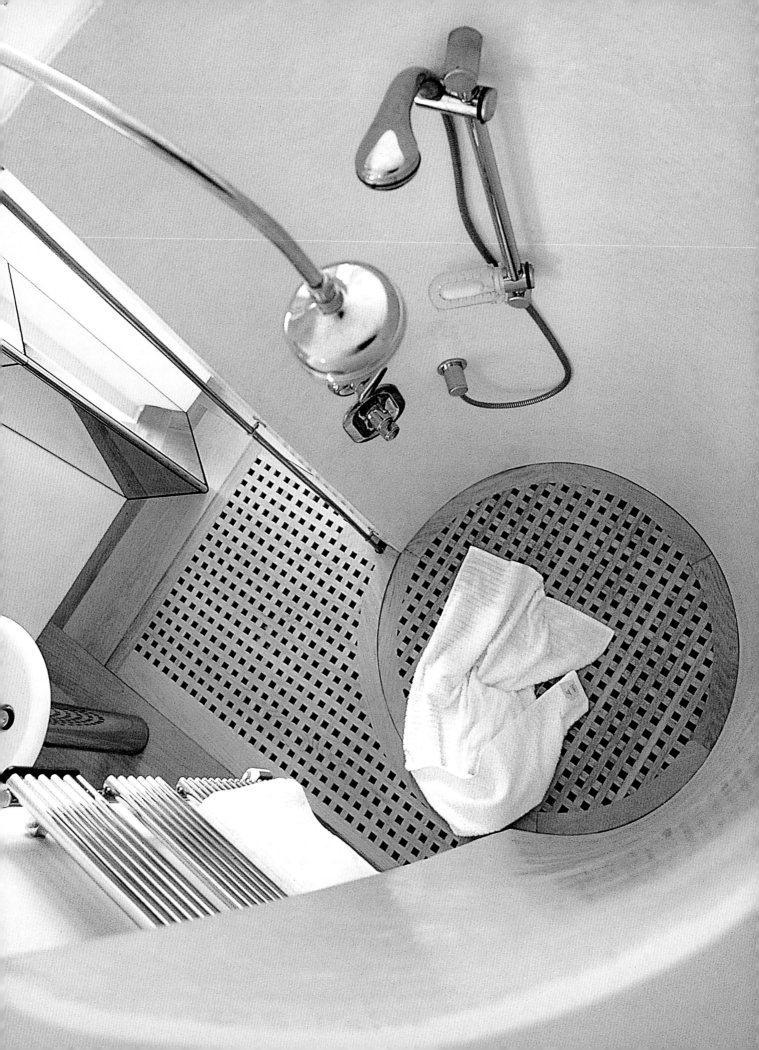

A freestanding wall separating bath and basin conceals the services, and also provides a degree of privacy within the open sleeping and bathing quarters. Similarly, the shower alcove is contained but feels part of the room.

Techno Futurism

This open-plan apartment, located on the top floor of a substantial farmhouse that has been absorbed into the suburbs of Brescia, was designed by Vincenzo De Cotiis for a music producer and is so sleekly futuristic as to be reminiscent of a James Bond or Austin Powers film set – a serious play pad.

Although the sleeping and bathing areas are effectively an open-plan extension of the living quarters, space is modulated so that different areas are designated for different purposes. As you enter the apartment, the sleeping and bathing area is partly concealed by a screen, guiding visitors away from the more private areas towards the living quarters. The bed and double-sized bath face each other, while a wall divides the bath and basin and the shower is partly enclosed in an alcove. Also part of the suite are a separate lavatory and gym. On the washbasin side the wall is highly polished stainless steel, so that the reflective surface can be used as a mirror.

In keeping with the sleek styling and materials, the bathing equipment is state of the art. The bath itself can be concealed by a cover. Inside, it has two compartments with separate controls operated on flip-up screens, allowing two people to use different jacuzzi and massage jet functions at the same time. The shower is enclosed in a three-sided alcove so that it is feels open to the room but the water is contained, and the floor slopes to a drain in the middle. As well as the central overhead shower, jets of water from the side create the aquatic equivalent of surround sound.

Bathing Platform

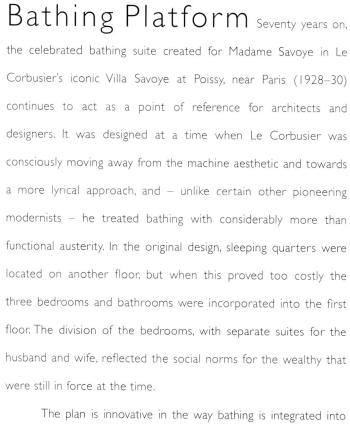

Seventy years on, the celebrated bathing suite created for Madame Savoye in Le Corbusier's iconic Villa Savoye at Poissy, near Paris (1928–30) continues to act as a point of reference for architects and designers. It was designed at a time when Le Corbusier was consciously moving away from the machine aesthetic and towards a more lyrical approach, and – unlike certain other pioneering modernists – he treated bathing with considerably more than functional austerity. In the original design, sleeping quarters were located on another floor, but when this proved too costly the three bedrooms and bathrooms were incorporated into the first floor. The division of the bedrooms, with separate suites for the husband and wife, reflected the social norms for the wealthy that were still in force at the time.

The plan is innovative in the way bathing is integrated into the sleeping quarters. The bathroom itself is effectively a box within the larger bedroom space. At one end is a bidet and basin, while the tiled bathing area containing the bath and sculptural *chaise longue* can be either open to the bedroom or closed off behind a curtain. The bathing area consists of a raised platform with the separate elements – the sunken bath and curvacious day bed – tiled so that they merge into the floor, as if it were a sort of furnished landscape. The *chaise-longue* is positioned near the ribbon window so that the bather can enjoy the view and light from the south façade.

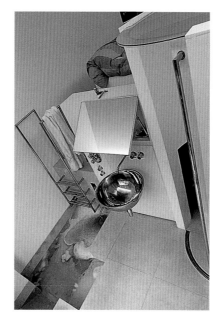

The open bathing area is a raised platform with a sunken bath lined in tiles of Portuguese limestone specially treated for water resistance. The mirror opens upwards to reveal storage. The lavatory is in the cylinder.

Spatial Games
In this comparatively small loft apartment in a former industrial building, architect Mark Guard accommodated the client's request for two bedrooms by dividing the space and interweaving functions with the complexity of a Chinese puzzle.

A vast white canvas screen can be rolled across the entrance wall to close off the rear of the apartment and create a sense of privacy in the master suite. Behind this, spaces for sleeping, bathing and dressing are dovetailed together with stairs and ladders and the use of different levels, to make a sort of sculptural adventure playground. The bed is raised on a platform above a walk-in wardrobe. Sandwiched behind this, and beside a large window, is the bathing area. Instead of a regular bath, there is more or less a mini-pool in the form of a staggered cross, so there are corners to lean against. It can be reached directly from the bed via a swimming pool ladder. Next door to it, a Tardis-like cylinder with a curved door houses the lavatory. The spare bedroom, or rather bed, is also housed on a platform, this time raised above a shower and guest toilet and reached by a staircase with staggered steps.

INDOORS/OUTDOORS

In *Clock Shower*, a short film by the late Gordon Matta Clark, the artist methodically washes, shaves and brushes his teeth balanced on a giant clock face, while below him the world scurries to work. If this absurdist sketch is about reversing norms and disclosing private formalities in public, it also exposes the faintly ridiculous artifice of our so-called 'civilized' bathing habits once the veil of privacy has been lifted.

Somewhat ironically, the millennium years seem to be preoccupied with a yearning to shed redundant formalities and douse ourselves in nature, and bathing has become one of the focuses of this idealization of a more elemental existence – a means to restore contact with nature in a way which has been squeezed out of our mechanized, digitalized lives. In *Undesigning the Bath*, Leonard Koren exalts 'undesigned' bathing experiences created by natural geologic processes or, if man is involved, not trained architects or designers but what Koren describes as 'composers of sensory stimulation working in an intuitive, poetic open-minded-undesign-manner.'

This is part of the reason we are drawn to other bathing cultures. Rustic simplicity is essential to the authentic sauna, for example. In Japan, the presence of nature, a reminder of the hot spring, is a part of the ideal bathing experience even within the city, and until recently public bath houses invariably opened on to a garden, although now the pressure on space means this has often been reduced to a desultory tiled mosaic of Mount Fuji or some other reference to a familiar beauty spot. In everyday life, however, it is usually a question of reinventing the exhilaration of open-air bathing in a way that does not preclude the convenience of hot and cold running water. California's sybaritic outdoor bathing culture is built on the intersection of nature and artifice. Although the hot tub has its origins in the Japanese *rotenburo*, in Californian style it has been reinvented from a place of lone contemplation and comparatively innocent gathering, to become an emblem of a hedonistic, even orgiastic lifestyle.

Certain designers play with the juncture between indoors and outdoors to restore a sense of wonder to bathing. In John Lautner's futuristic Sheats residence (see pages 110-15), water and rich tropical vegetation dissolve the boundaries between interior and exterior. One of the most spectacular elements is a hand basin which is hardly more than a slit in a glass wall, so that you wash your hands in a futuristic waterfall gazing down on the city. In the suburbs of Sydney, Richard Leplastrier has broken the bathroom into its component parts and rearranged them so that the bathtub sits on the front porch (see pages 118-19).

But although a warm climate and geophysical resources are a benefit, there are outdoor traditions in cold countries as well. The exhilaration of contrasting extremes of temperatures is part of the thrill of the sauna and the Russian *bania*, where adepts cool off in freezing waters. Japanese outdoor hot springs are used all year, and in winter bathers lie in hot baths enjoying the snowy landscape. In Iceland's Blue Lagoon, water heated by a nuclear power station is pumped up from subterranean depths to a swimming pool that steams in winter.

There are other ways of domesticating the exhilaration of outdoor bathing. In South London, interior architect Charles Rutherfoord uses an outdoor shower on the rear balcony of a Victorian villa all year. It is positioned beside the indoor shower, so that you step directly from hot water indoors to hot water outdoors, and has a judiciously positioned 'modesty panel' to provide some privacy. In a London house designed by John Pawson, a motorized skylight can be opened so that you can shower directly under the stars, while in John Young's apartment on the Thames, bathers can soak in the river light and wide skies protected in a glass tower.

'THE CONTRAST BETWEEN THE CAVE-LIKE INTERIOR AND THE ANGULAR
GLASS EMPHASIZES THE STONE-AGE FUTURIST SENSIBILITY.'

Crystal Cavity
The late John Lautner,
a pupil of Frank Lloyd Wright, built a series of houses expounding
his dramatic vision of the Californian lifestyle that teeter
somewhere between cave dwelling and sci-fi. The Sheats/
Goldstein residence, designed in 1963 and remodelled in 1989, is
built high into the rocky mountainside above Beverley Hills, jutting
out from the cliffs to take advantage of spectacular views over Los
Angeles towards the Pacific Ocean. From the stream which you
cross at the entrance, to the swimming pool, to the bathing area in
the master bedroom suite which opens on to a terrace with a hot
tub, the celebration of water is thematic.

Lautner took advantage of the climate to dissolve
boundaries between indoors and outdoors. He had originally
designed the living area to be completely open, protected by an
invisible air curtain, but glass walls were added later. The master
suite on a lower floor below the pool terrace originally included a
bedroom, den and studio, but was remodelled for the current
owner to make a private suite with walls of frameless glass open
to the panoramic view. The contrast between the cave-like interior
with walls in rough-cast concrete and the angular glass perimeter
walls emphasizes the stone-age futurist sensibility, almost as if the

house were a crystal partially exposed in the hillside. The interior wall is pierced by three glowing jade-coloured windows looking underwater into the pool.

In the open-plan suite, the washing and dressing area adjoining the bedroom is structured by a series of dwarf walls which conceal the toilet and storage and serve as screens partially dividing the space. Lautner's fondness for geometry reaches an apotheosis in the bathing area, with its skewered trapezoid forms and views that slice through the concrete and glass. Water is introduced in unexpected ways. In one basin it appears by magic when you pass your hand below a mirror, activating a concealed sensor. The indoor shower is mirrored by an outdoor shower area on the other side of the glass wall on the decked private terrace, with a sunken hot-tub jacuzzi positioned so that you have the impression of floating in the view. Indoors, the shower taps set in concrete – designed by Lautner and custom-made – continue the angular, futuristic theme. The architect plays with a rich palette of extravagant and immaculately crafted materials, from the highly polished African granite streaked in pink and black to the rich, dark wood of the terrace, as well as concrete and glass.

But the single most spectacular element is the abstraction of a washbasin that is little more than a slot in the glass wall. When a sensor is activated a sheet of water falls from the arm-like spout and runs away down the outside of the sloping glass wall. The effect is like washing your hands in a natural cascade, while enjoying the staggering view.

In the bathing area, functional elements are rigorously concealed in sculptural abstraction. The basin is built into the granite counter and water appears from behind the floating mirror when a concealed sensor is activated.

Tub with a View

Pretty much the first thing visitors see when they arrive at this house in Pittwater, north Sydney, and climb the steps to the front porch is the wooden bathtub positioned on the large deck which functions as an open-air living room. If placing the bath on public view as nonchalantly as if it were a rocking chair seems a radical gesture – at least to those used to bourgeois ideas of propriety (and prurience) – here architect Richard Leplastrier reverses many of the accepted domestic norms, rethinking what constitutes living space to suit a particular way of life.

In the Osborne house, cooking and bathing are at the heart of the home, making what were once considered private activites public and acknowledging that in contemporary households these can be sociable epicentres of home life. From the tub, bathers can converse with cook or guests in the kitchen or on the terrace. The shower and lavatory are housed in cubicles behind.

The presence of water is especially important in a hot climate. Pools or basins positioned at the entrance to buildings are common in many cultures – whether fountains or the impressively simple square of water sometimes found beside a mosque, which may be used for ritual ablutions and also acts as a temperature regulator in courtyards.

Built from recycled wood, marine plywood and corrugated plastic and metal, the 'light' materials and sense of impermanence reflect Leplastrier's interest in ecologically sound buildings and his knowledge of boat building, while also recalling the simple structures and materials of Australian townships. Like a boat, the house can be opened up by a series of hatches so that domestic life can extend outdoors or be enclosed, depending on the weather.

The shower units by Stella, incorporating taps and exposed piping, are made for use outdoors and wherever plumbing cannot be sunk in the wall.

Sightseeing
Although a northern European urban rooftop is not – in theory, at least – the most conducive place for an outdoor shower, there is little reason why with a good supply of hot water it shouldn't work for more than the few fairweather weeks. On the rooftop of this Parisian apartment, where Les Invalides, the Eiffel Tower and countless other monuments can be pointed out like a tour guide spinning round a diorama, the shower becomes another way to enjoy the vista, a place to cool off after sunbathing or for kids to play.

The chimney block is used as a support for the pair of shower units. The basins are tinned trays, traditionally made for baking large cakes by a metal workshop in Tunis. The mats are also made in Tunisia, for use on the floor and walls in mosques and homes. When the bowls fill up, you simply empty them over the roof.

The freestanding bathing tower built from Luxcrete glass bricks in a steel frame is reached by a bridge from the mezzanine sleeping level. The concrete platform is warmed by underfloor heating, and the tower is heated by industrial fins.

Bathroom Tower

The bathroom in, or rather on, architect John Young's apartment beside the Thames at Hammersmith – a glass tower on a cinematic roofline – could almost be described as a high-tech folly. By day it shimmers in the river light, and by night glows enigmatically in the dark. Inside, bathers are submerged in broad skies and strong light.

That Young should indulge a passion for the functional and poetic possibilities of industrial engineering in his own apartment is hardly surprising. One of the team of three that founded the Richard Rogers partnership, Young helped build Beaubourg and Lloyds. He admires the refined detailing in the aircraft and boat-building industries, and the way such structures can be attuned to the climate, and describes the apartment as 'a celebration of precision and detail, how the whole can be shaped by the details.'

The bath tower is a freestanding building joined to the main block by a bridge and entered through a curved glass door. Young cites gasometers and oil storage tanks as inspiration for the cylindrical form and the way the ramp spirals around the exterior. The glass brick wall is braced inside to withstand high winds.

In Young's inventive approach to detailing, industrial parts have been adapted and domesticated: 'nothing is concealed and so everything has to be properly designed.' The room is heated by an industrial finned tube running around the wall beside a rank of gleaming stainless steel pipes. Heating coils embedded in the concrete make it warm to the touch, and it is polished to create a gentler surface. The grills surrounding the bath drain any water spilling out of the tub. The taps are designed for institutional use, as are the surgical sinks incorporating ledges and the stainless steel lavatory, while the bidet has been made by customizing another lavatory. The cedarwood tub was made in Japan and can be covered when not in use. The circular mirrors designed by Eileen Gray and the shower frames playfully echo the geometry of the building.

DATABASE

Alongside the kitchen, the bathroom is usually the most complex and costly room in the house, and the hardest to change once it has been completed as it deals with fixed supplies and waste. Technical requirements are considerable – there is nothing more tedious than a leaking pipe or a shower without adequate hot water – and regulations concerning sanitation and hot and cold water supplies, central heating, drainage, ventilation and electrics are necessarily strict and vary from country to country.

In the last 20 years, the choice of what is available in sanitary ware and fittings, as well as technologies for baths, showers and steam rooms, has grown considerably, but bathroom planning is still hindered by the structure of the industry, where one manufacturer makes baths, another taps, and so on. Although suppliers are learning from developments in the kitchen industry and linking together to market complementary ranges to help streamline the design process, it is still often a question of piecing together parts from different ranges and the customer is continually left asking whether or not this bit works with that.

Equally, fittings do not necessarily cross frontiers easily. In the UK, where water pressure is lower than in the United States and Continental Europe, many fittings can require the use of a pump to boost pressure. These can either be installed for individual fittings such as a power shower, or to service a particular room or even the whole house. Essential questions to ask are, 'Do I have enough water for what I want to do?' and, 'Are the various fittings compatible?' Lavatories also work differently in different countries, and you should always check with the supplier.

Existing plumbing arrangements, such as the positioning of the soil stack and water supplies, can be determining factors in planning a bathroom. Beyond the choice of sanitary and hardware, space planning, heating, ventilation, lighting, storage,

materials, mirrors and accessories are just some of the issues that need to be considered.

For all these reasons, specialist help is pretty much essential in the bathroom. Showrooms can give advice on planning and choosing fittings, but do not necessarily provide an installation service. Hiring an architect or designer, who takes charge of the whole process of design and installation, should – in theory, at least – remove headaches.

One factor of bathroom planning to consider is how a bathroom or bathing facilities will be used, by how many people and when. Unconventional solutions that suit one person or a couple might not work in a family home. While current thinking tends towards more individual facilities linked to bedrooms – even two bathrooms linked to the master bedroom – this depends on space and budget, and the alternative of communal facilities can make a home a more sociable place.

While planners have established certain groupings and minimum bathroom dimensions – citing 3 sq m for a bath and basin, 4 sq m for bath, basin and lavatory, 4.5 sq m with a bidet and 7 sq m including a shower – in Japan bathrooms for small apartments are designed to fit into cupboards. As many of the bathrooms in this book show, conventions can happily be turned around, and solutions determined by sanitary engineers drilled on ergonomics are not necessarily the most enjoyable or even practical. Although money can help, a large budget is certainly no guarantee of a pleasurable or even workable bathroom – most important of all, the bathroom requires intelligent planning.

This database cannot attempt to be comprehensive, but is concerned with the ideas and aesthetics of the bathrooms featured in this book, offering some alternative solutions and pointing out some of the technical aspects to take into consideration.

MATERIALS

For much of the twentieth century the bathroom was a place where cleanliness and practicality came first and materials and surfaces were chosen to be waterproof, wipeable, tough and impervious to staining above all else. Today, however, other issues to do with the enjoyment of the senses and surface and texture – what a stone or wood floor feels like to walk on barefoot, for example – are also valued, and there are now considerably more options than just tiling.

As many of the bathrooms in this book reveal, the current trend is towards natural materials chosen for the way they look and feel, as well as the way they wear – usually getting more beautiful with age. How a material reacts with water is an important consideration, although perhaps not always in the way we think: while some cultures protect wood against exposure to water with layers of varnish, the Japanese tub or bath house floor is allowed to soften and eventually disintegrate with age. Certain materials or combinations associated with modern interiors, such as stainless steel and glass, can appear hard-edged and uninviting in the bathroom, bringing to mind the laboratory or surgery.

The choice of materials also depends on the climate. Wood is especially warm and inviting in a cold climate, whereas large expanses of ceramic tiles may be more suitable in a warmer country, where the slight coolness is refreshing. Increasing use of underfloor heating is making a huge difference, particularly with 'colder' materials like stone, tiles or concrete.

Marble and stone

Two of the most luxurious materials traditionally associated with water and bathing are stone and marble. From the Roman *thermae* to the Islamic hamam, marble in particular has been valued for its glacial smoothness and translucency, and used to evoke wealth and splendour. More recently, in reaction to marble's association with ostentation and glitz, many architects and designers have fought shy of using it over large areas, tending to prefer more sober and restrained limestones and sandstones in pared-down modern interiors and, similarly, matt or rough textures over the highly polished. Ecologists advise using local stones wherever possible.

In the London bathroom (see pages 64-69), the floor is paved in York stone and the same stone is used for benches, the bath and the sculptural basin, which is carved out of a solid block. The walls are finished in a waterproof cement mixed to match the dark, sandy colour of the stone. In the loft apartment (see pages 106-7), light creamy white Portuguese limestone tiles are used for the floor throughout, including the bathing area and even the sunken bath. In the Los Angeles bathroom (see pages 76-77), large slate tiles are used on the floor, the blue-grey matching the graphite-coloured plaster on walls and bath. In the Paris apartment (see pages 72-73), the barrel-vaulted room lined with rough-textured granite walls is reminiscent of the dark solemnity of some Aztec ruin. The use of stone for walls as well as floors gives a bathroom unity – at a price, of course.

When marble is used, it tends to be simply detailed or follow utilitarian traditions, to play down the neo-classical associations with florid splendour. The basin designed by Piero Lissoni for Boffi recalls the way marble was used in dairies, as does the washing trough (pic 2). In the New York penthouse (see pages 58-61), polished and highly

1

2

3

4

5

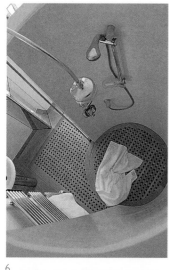

6

7

Photographs:
1 Polished concrete and a sculptural marble basin in a bathroom designed by Seth Stein.
2 Marble trough by John Pawson.
3 Large bath in contrasting colours of marble by Al Sayed and Fink, a modern take on antique forms.
4 The counter with a sunken basin is in the same stripy granite as the floor.
5 Bath and walls are finished in slate-coloured pool plaster.
6 In this freestanding shower, the walls are covered in Armourcoat waterproof plaster.
7 In this shower room in Kenya, the walls are finished in contrasting earthy-coloured plasters.

patterned contrasting marbles recall antique examples, yet the lines and detailing are determinedly modern. In the bathroom marble is used in large slabs, whereas the shower is lined entirely with smaller square tiles laid to form a chequerboard effect. Equally luxurious is the use of a highly polished and patterned African granite (a hard, durable stone that is weather resistant and impervious to water) in the Sheats residence in Los Angeles (see pages 110-15), contrasting with the rough texture of the cast-concrete walls.

Hamam builders were masters of marble and there is a lot we can learn from them – for instance, in the way marble or stone is heated from beneath as in the Roman *thermae*, a precursor to modern underfloor heating systems.

Stones should be chosen according to use as well as looks, although durability also depends on

fixing and finishing, and you should always take advice from the supplier and use a skilled installer. In the past decade, sealing products have improved enormously and the same silicone-based impregnator can be used on a bathroom floor as on kitchen or general flooring. The sealant appears matt and allows the stone to age, which, after all, is the point of natural materials. While water does no harm to stone, the idea is to protect it against other stains such as bathroom products or coffee. For areas which are likely to be wet continually, such as vanity tops, shower trays, bath surrounds or indeed baths, specialists recommend a resin-based sealant which is applied by the masons cutting the stone.

On the other hand, as one stone merchant pointed out, many architects, contractors and clients make a big fuss over finishes and treating stones, whereas in, say, a Mediterranean seaside house stone might be left untreated in its natural state and allowed to darken with age, adding to its character and beauty. One pleasing aspect about not sealing stone is the way it changes colour with water and shows up wet footprints. The question is whether you compromise appearance for practicality or practicality for appearance.

Slipperiness is another issue. Again, this depends on the nature and surface of the stone and how far you are prepared to compromise appearance for safety. Polished marble or granite will be much more slippery than a relatively open-faced

stone such as a Burgundy limestone. Surfaces can be roughed up by processes such as flaming or honing, or slate riven to make it slip resistant.

Depending on the building structure, weight can be an important consideration with marble and stone used over large areas. Marble and granite 'veneers' have been developed for weight-specific situations such as on ships and planes: the stone is bonded to a lightweight high-tech material and then ground down to a thin veneer.

In bathrooms where luxury is equated with simplicity and solid, natural materials, sinks and even baths may be made from stone or marble, often recalling antique forms. In the Pawson bathroom, the basin is a hemisphere scooped out of a solid block, while the bath is constructed from five panels with reinforcing bars in the corners. Claudio Silvestrin has recently designed i fiumi, a stone range for Boffi made by Italian craftsmen including basins shaped like bowls and a large circular bath.

Plaster and concrete

Certains types of plaster have been used to make buildings weatherproof since ancient times, and the Romans lined their aqueducts and water cisterns with this material. The surface can be deliciously smooth to touch; it can be used to make sculptural forms, and coloured to virtually any shade. In the New York loft apartment (see pages 48-51), the bathroom is a sculptural blue island finished in polished blue plaster to give a surface that feels like stone. The wooden form was built in sections lined inside with fibreglass, and covered with layers of plaster built up to about 1 cm thick. The plaster was waxed and polished to achieve a smooth, reflective surface. Because it is a solid colour, chips are scarcely visible. In the Los Angeles bathroom (see pages 76-77), the bath is finished in a waterproof Venetian plaster made for use in swimming pools. Liquid and solid beeswax polishes can be used on plaster and stone to make a durable waterproof surface, but you should seek advice or test an area first.

In the Bath apartment (see pages 98-99), the sculptural wall concealing the shower is finished in travertine-coloured Armourcoat, a proprietary waterproof plaster made using marble dust. Other similar products are available.

Old-fashioned lime paints such as gypsum, traditionally used to protect the exteriors of houses, can also be used inside on bathroom walls. The advantage is that, unlike synthetic paints, they allow the walls to breathe.

In the deckhouse (see pages 124-7), the concrete floor is polished to give a softer surface. Concrete can also be used for casting baths, basins and other furnishings like counters and shelves; however, weight should be taken into consideration if it is to be used in any quantity.

There are also lightweight concrete alternatives. Syndecrete, developed by Los Angeles-based Syndesis, is a cement-based composite using natural minerals such as volcanic ash, which is half the weight and has twice the compressive strength of standard concrete. It feels much like stone and can be used for custom-made pre-cast tubs, sinks, counters and other bathroom fittings.

Tiles

Ceramic tiles have long been standard issue for bathrooms, stressing the hygienic and waterproof requirements. The hard, shiny surface of glazed tiles is extremely durable, resistant to stains, easily cleaned, scratchproof and so on. They also reflect light in a way that can be helpful in a small room.

Tiles come in an immense variety of shapes, sizes, colours and patterns, but the effect is in the detailing as well as the tile itself, and it is worth using an experienced tiler for all but the simplest jobs. Large expanses of plain tiling can be rather forbidding, recalling hospitals and institutions, and for this reason ceramic and glass mosaic tiles with an uneven surface that shimmers in the light have become a popular alternative. As with other materials, the current fashion is for simplicity and unity. Colourwise, blues and greens work particularly well in bathrooms for their refreshing qualities and associations with water.

The bog-standard square white tile is the most basic and economic format. Industrial tiles, like the rectangular white tiles made for use in underground railway systems and industrial and institutional buildings, are also economic and extremely durable. A tougher-quality tile is generally used for floors with a non-slip surface. In the Los Angeles shower room (see pages 74-75), white floor tiles give the room a utilitarian feeling. In the Chucho Reyes bathroom (see pages 52-53), large-format tiles are used for the walls and floor, and they also cover the walls and steps leading down into the bathing area, creating the effect of a sunken room.

Small, square tiles that have a similar effect to mosaic were used by early modernists and have enjoyed a huge revival in popularity recently. They are supplied in sheets, so are relatively easy to lay. Such tiles come in different qualities and a huge range of colours, including many different whites and metallic colours. Most

1

2

3

4

expensive are the Venetian glass mosaic tiles. Their beauty lies in the almost gem-like slight translucence, and the way light plays on the uneven surfaces. A cheaper quality that is more dense and matt in appearance is made for use in swimming pools, and these are supplied in plain colours or patterned panels. In the Glass House bathroom (see pages 70-71), the cylindrical capsule is lined with green mosaic tiles, creating an intense experience of colour. The shower tray is simply a rounded ridge built into the tiled floor, echoing the circular form of the room.

Hexagonal tiles are standard in America, used in countless commercial buildings. Off-white hexagonal tiles are used for the floors in the Parr and New York lofts (see pages 86-89 and 54-57) and in the small cloakroom in Los Angeles (see pages 80-81), where they cover floors, walls and ceiling.

There are also qualities of tile with less highly glazed and unglazed surfaces. In Le Corbusier's bathroom for Madame Savoye (see pages 104-5), the bathing area is a raised platform with a sunken pool lined in handmade blue tiles and a serpentine chaise covered in similar stone-coloured tiles. The uneven surface and variations in colour give them a life and softness not associated with manufactured tiles. In contrast, the walls of the 'bathing box' are covered in more utilitarian, highly glazed horizontal white tiles.

In the country house outside Paris (see pages 92-97), Masakazu Bokura uses traditional unglazed terracotta floor tiles for the bedroom and bathing area. There is a warmth about the worn, pitted surface of old tiles – it is worth searching out salvaged versions.

As in the kitchen, tiles can be used to cover counters and structural units. Andrée Putman uses white tiles to cover a long counter which is the spine of the bathroom (see page 35), with bath and basin built into it rather like a kitchen counter, giving something of the utilitarian washdown look of a laboratory, but softened by the accessories. The undercounter storage consists of open shelves which are also tiled.

The effect of tiling is created not just by the tile itself but also by the grouting, which can be discreet or contrasting. In pic 6 turquoise-blue mosaic tiles are used with white grouting.

Dutch designer collective Droog have come up with a clever play on the universal and utilitarian format of the standard white tile, producing a range of tile-sized accessories that can be inserted into a tiled bathroom. These include not only mirror tiles but also tiles incorporating shaver plugs, small drawers, tissue holders, mini-televisions to catch news or sport while you shave, radios and other useful and entertaining versions.

Photographs:
1 Hexagonal tiles used on walls and floors create a honeycomb effect.
2 Standard-format white tiles used to cover walls and built-in counter.
3 Square glass mosaic tiles in jade-green almost give the effect of being underwater.
4 Unglazed terracotta floor tiles are warm and natural in appearance, and look better with age.
5 Rectangular glass wall tiles in different blues laid in an irregular pattern.
6 Contrasting white grouting used with blue mosaic on walls, floor and freestanding washbasin unit, plus the bath panel.
7 Grouting tends to turn grey with age, especially on floors.
8 Droog's functional tiles. Clockwise from top left: medicine drawer in a red cross, towel hook, shaver plug and tissue holder.

5

6

7

8

Wood

The appeal of wood is its softness and warmth to the touch and the way in which it mellows with age. In Japanese bath houses, where wood is traditionally used for every surface from floors and walls to the tub itself, there is a deeply soothing, insulating, restorative quality. Similarly, saunas are traditionally built entirely from wood which is untreated, so that the chemicals from varnish do not contaminate the steam. Wood is also a natural regulator of the indoor climate which 'breathes' and stabilizes humidity. Equally, the use of wood in bathrooms recalls boat-building traditions that can be both practical and elegant.

Although wood has been used comparatively little in western bathing environments, where more obviously durable surfaces are favoured, this is beginning to change as the gentle characteristics of wood are increasingly appreciated. Hasseludden, a new spa centre near Stockholm, for instance, draws on Japanese and Scandinavian traditions to create an environment where wood is used extensively – for the pool, exercise areas, restaurants etc – giving it a tranquillity not often associated with the hard surfaces of communal bathing environments.

Different woods are perishable to varying degrees, and the type of wood should be chosen carefully for its compatibility with water – the extensive use of wood in marine industries is evidence that certain woods coexist happily with water. Many woods suitable for exterior use can also be employed in the bathroom. On the whole, hardwoods are more durable than softwoods; when selecting, you should ensure that all woods, but especially tropical hardwoods, are produced from sustainable sources.

One of the cheapest forms of wood for bathroom use is sheet plywood. Part of the current trend for using industrial materials admired for their utilitarian, factory-made appearance, it can nevertheless be lifted from its relatively humble origins – as some of the bathrooms in this book show. Marine ply is made for use on boats and is bonded using a waterproof glue. More economic still are exterior grades of ply that are moisture-resistant and give protection against humidity and splashing. Plywood comes in a range of veneers and can be protected by sealing with a polyurethene varnish.

In the Langlands and Bell bathroom (see pages 82-85), the room was constructed using a softwood frame and lined in varnished birch ply, which is also used to panel the bath and for the floor, giving the room a unity and warmth that makes it feel rather like being inside a cabinet. The lavatory seat made by Langlands and Bell is also in ply. In the Sporre bathroom (see pages 42-47), marine ply is used for both the storage wall with sliding doors and the low wall on the opposite side of the room which conceals the plumbing, and is made in panels which can be removed for access. A long, sunken shelf let into the wall contains and partially conceals bathroom products and utensils. In contrast to the ply walls, the limed oak floor and aged patina of the wooden bath show how different woods can be made to work together to give a rich palette of natural colours.

In the small Mizrahi bathroom (see pages 78-79), the walls are clad in ash plywood chosen for its flamboyant grain. The wood has been finished with a high-gloss lacquer used in the marine industry, so that it is highly reflective and almost looks as if it is wet and rippling.

Tongue-and-groove or wainscotting is another comparatively reasonable solution. In both the Parr bathroom and New York loft (see pages 86-89 and 54-57), painted tongue-and-groove panelling is fitted to above head height, creating a sense of warm enclosure within the raw industrial spaces as well as concealing pipework. To protect against moisture, panelling should

1

2

3

4

be painted using a product suitable for exterior use or boat paints.

Certain solid timbers can be used in the bathroom. Cedar is resistant to rot and is used outdoors for roof shingles, decking and so on. Teak and mahogany are both used in the boat-building industry and are available from sustainable sources. Hardwoods such as teak are frequently used in areas where surfaces are likely to be soaked regularly, such as bath surrounds and shower floors.

In the Bath shower room (see pages 98-99), the small area of the shower floor is fitted with a teak deck custom-made by a ship's carpenter. The platform extends beyond the shower enclosure, to make space for drying without dripping across the bedroom floor. The Osborne house (see pages 116-121) is largely constructed from recycled wood and plywood, and in the bathroom area different woods are used for particular purposes: ply for the wall panels, including the

portholes and shutters, while the floors and deck are solid timber. Like the deck, the tub has weathered to a soft silver-grey.

JAPANESE TUBS

The Japanese wooden bath is an oriental tradition that has recently been adopted in the west. Woods used for baths are chosen to release a scent when wet - usually Japanese cypress or Chinese black pine, although Japanese cedar and chestnut are also used. In *onsen* hot spring resorts, communal wooden baths can be as large as small swimming pools (see pages 22-23), and before it was easy to heat large quantities of water at home, communal steam rooms – often attached to monasteries – were built for public use and were also constructed from wood. Simple circular baths are made from planks held together in metal bands rather like half-barrels, a form sometimes borrowed for hot tubs.

Although the wooden tub was common a century ago, today traditional baths are costly to make and comparatively rare, and are mainly found in *onsen* or traditional *ryokan* inns. One maker in Kyoto, who has been declared a national living treasure for his skill, is deluged with orders for years ahead. Wooden baths require special care. To prevent shrinkage and therefore leaking, baths should be kept filled if not used regularly. With use the wood begins to soften and disintegrate, so baths have to be replaced periodically. Outside Japan, a good cabinet maker should be able to make you a wooden tub.

Photographs:
1 Painted tongue-and-groove panelling.
2 A room within a room, constructed from birch ply.
3 In this bathroom different woods are used – limed oak for the floor, marine ply for the false wall – creating a warm palette of natural materials.
4 Wood used for bathroom floors is pleasurable to walk on.
5 Hardwoods such as teak can be used for indoor and outdoor shower floors.
6 Sea creatures carved in the planks of a deck.

5

6

Glass

Glass is one of the most innovative building materials of the twentieth century and is most intimately associated with chic modernity in bathrooms, transparency having a natural affinity to water. New developments in the glass industry have furnished architects with materials possessing unexpected and sometimes extraordinary qualities, allowing designers to optimize natural light and create enclosures with minimal severance or intrusion, playing with ideas of transparency and exposure.

The variety of different glasses available in terms of colour, degree of translucency or opacity and performance is huge. Recent technological developments include glass that filters certain rays, photosensitive glass that changes with light intensity, and glass that allows those on the inside to see out but appears opaque to those looking in, as well as astonishing glass that can be changed from clear to opaque at the flick of a switch. Such developments help overcome problems associated with an extensive use of glass, such as the need for privacy, protection from sunlight, heat loss and so on.

While ordinary glass is extremely fragile, tempered or safety glass is considerably stronger and if broken disintegrates into relatively harmless fragments. Laminated safety glass consists of two or more glass panes laminated to plastic, so that if it cracks the glass sticks to the tough plastic. Panels of laminated glass are used by architectural designer Charles Rutherfoord (pic 4) for the floor of a raised bathing platform to display a collection of shells and pebbles which is illuminated at night.

In the SoHo loft apartment (see pages 48-51) designed by Archi-tectonics, the bathroom is enclosed by custom-made glass walls consisting of a Japanese glass product composed of a film sandwiched between two layers of glass held in a stainless steel frame. According to designer Winka Dubbeldam, this particular glass was chosen for its qualities of translucency, appearing less dense than conventional sandblasted glass. From the living quarters on the other side of the wall, the glass acts like a screen – silhouettes of bathers are just visible, rather like a muffled shadow puppet show.

In a Los Angeles bathroom by architect Brian Murphy (pic 2), the basin area and shower room are housed in a tank-like glass box installed within the master suite. The greenish hues of the opaque glass, which change in the artificial light, contrive a sensation of being submerged underwater which is appropriate to bathing.

There are many different qualities of etched and sandblasted glass with different levels of transparency and hues ranging from milky white to almost jade-green. Obvious applications are for bathroom windows or walls where light and privacy are required or to

1

2

3

4

screen an ugly view. In a London apartment designed by architect Philip Gumuchdjian (pics 7 and 8), an opaque glass wall divides the shower from the kitchen, allowing natural light into an internal bathroom and animating the kitchen with discreet shadows of bathers. Glass is frequently used for shower enclosures and doors, as in the Manhattan apartment (see pages 58-61), and for steam-room doors, letting in light and minimizing claustrophobia. Where feasible, skylights can be used in a similar way to flood internal areas with light and open bathrooms to the outside world while protecting privacy.

In John Lautner's Sheats residence (see pages 110-15), the master suite leading on to a deck surrounded by vegetation is enclosed in angular, frameless glass walls, blurring the boundaries between indoors and outdoors. The shower room is housed in a projecting glass box with a sloping glass roof, creating a feeling almost like showering

outdoors but protected from the elements. The most spectacular feature is the abstracted glass basin, where a sheet of water falls from a projecting spout on the inside and flows out down the exterior of the sloping glass wall. In such installations, the rippling patterns of water running over glass and the steamy effects of condensation are part of the drama.

In the Californian bathroom (see pages 76-77), sliding glass walls inside and leading on to the deck enclose the wet cell, reducing the sense of enclosure and allowing the small room to be opened up in good weather so that, again, it almost feels like bathing outdoors.

Such special glass products as glass bricks and glass tubing for walls were exploited structurally by early Modernists. In architect John Young's London apartment (see pages 124-27), the bathroom is housed in a tower built from Luxcrete glass bricks in a steel frame braced from within against strong winds. The clear

roof consists of double-glazed roof panels by Pilkington. All too often, though, walls of glass bricks inserted for no particular reason have become a cliché of developers' mishmash Modernist aspirations.

The recent development of Privalite, a glass product which can be switched from clear to opaque, contrives dramatic possibilities for vicariously voyeuristic now-you-see-it-now-you-don't scenarios, playfully subverting accepted codes of privacy. The use of such glass for the bathroom walls in a bar in SoHo, which changed from clear to opaque on occupation, ensured crowds of gawpers. New York architect Michael Gabellini has used this glass for a private bathroom cube in a Manhattan apartment, flipping usual ideas of modesty on their head.

Glass can also be used to dazzling sculptural effect. The semi-circular glass bath designed by Masakazu Bokura (see pages 72 and 94-95) was custom-made from toughened glass by French master

glass craftsmen G. Saalburg and Desserne. Increasingly, glass is being used for washbasins, which play with transparency and take up less space visually than those constructed from more conventional solid materials.

5

6

7

8

HARDWARE

Washbasins

As well as being an essential component of the bathroom, the basin has become the nearest this room gets to a fashion item, mutating into all sorts of materials, forms and indeed other objects. If it has ritual associations with fonts and fountains, a basin filled with water is a mirror to the face. As well as shape, it should be about the material and what it is like when wet.

Key considerations are taps and plumbing. Increasingly, the use of wall-mounted taps and spouts or taps set in a surround is liberating the basin as well as the bath. With pedestal basins or half-pedestals, plumbing is concealed in the pedestal, while with basins set into or sitting on a counter or storage unit, plumbing is hidden in the unit just as in a kitchen. If plumbing is visible, be sure not to use ugly plastic waste pipes; these are available in stainless steel or

other finishes to match taps. In a glass room (pic 10) the tangle of pipes deliberately animates the cool design.

The standard basin height is usually 815 mm from floor to rim, although there is no reason to follow this and for taller people it can be back-strainingly low. Back specialists advise that basin and mirror should be at a height where you don't have to lean down to wash your face, shave or apply make-up.

The high-tech movement popularized the sourcing of non-domestic sanitary ware, plundered from institutional ranges. Many manufacturers make basins intended for commercial use, including ceramic and stainless steel troughs or utilitarian laboratory and surgery sinks, like those in the Langlands and Bell studio and Young's deckhouse (see pages 82-85 and 124-27).

Another economical solution is the traditional butler's sink. A number of designers, including Piero Lissoni, have reworked and domesticated such generic forms. Philippe Starck's

1

2

5

6

9

10

11

12

3

4

7

8

13

14

ceramic basin for Duravit is an update of the traditional washbowl, which before plumbing simply sat on a dresser or table top, and comes in a version with a washstand. In the Morabito house (pic 12), the basin is a stone bowl resting on a stone shelf.

In the hands of certain architects and designers, the basin has taken on monumental sculptural form. John Pawson's carved stone basins (see page 8) recall the simple and massive forms of ancient basins and fonts, investing washing with ritual that has been largely squeezed out of contemporary life. Claudio Silvestrin's designs for the i fiumi range are also carved from solid stone. With the development of laser cutting, in theory almost any shape can be cut from stone – at a price.

As in kitchens, metal, especially stainless steel and nickel-plated chrome, is widely used in the bathroom. Andrée Putman's design for Nito incorporates a metal bowl in an elegantly skeletal metal frame. Alternatively, a stainless steel bowl can sit on or be sunk into a counter, with a hole made to fit the waste.

Spectacular basins can be custom-made in toughened or tempered glass, as in the Sheats residence, where the basin is incorporated in a glass wall, or the concave glass basin by Brian Murphy (pic 10), with its exposed tangle of pipes. Agape manufacture a range of glass basins in different colours.

Recently, designers have been experimenting with unexpected materials for basins. Hella Jongerius' squashy resin basin for Droog defies

expectations by turning a hard object into something soft and squeezable. Boffi also produce a semi-transparent Ekotek resin basin (pic 2). Agape make a conical basin in veneered and sealed plywood that looks like a fruit bowl (pic 8).

The fact is that pretty much anything that can contain water can be used as a basin. In one Los Angeles home, Brian Murphy wittily used a galvanized pail plumbed neatly into a tree stump (see pages 74-75).

Photographs:

1 Institutional steel basin.

2 and 3 Two basins designed by Piero Lissoni for Boffi, the first in Ekotek, a fibreglass resin, and the second in ceramic.

4 Skeletal washstand by Andrée Putman for Nito.

5 Freestanding wash unit incorporating mirror and basin.

6 Outdoor stone basin.

7 Transparent acrylic basin in the Paul Rudolph house.

8 Conical wooden basin by Agape.

9 Wash by Vincent van Duysen from Obumex.

10 A dip in the glass shelf serves as a basin in a glass bathroom by Brian Murphy.

11 Box, from Agape, combines marble basin and wood cabinet.

12 A carved stone bowl on a stone shelf in Jacqueline Morabito's house.

13 Many current basins follow the simple, functional forms of the generic butler's sink.

14 Scola from Duravit, designed for use in schools, hospitals and other institutional buildings, incorporates a wide ledge.

Baths

The standard western bath was already cheaply mass-produced by 1910. This was a more or less coffin-shaped, one-person tub about 165 cm long, with either parallel or tapered sides, a rolled rim and taps attached, the bath itself being made of cast iron and enamelled on the inside. Although today the standard is pretty much the same, there are many more variations in shape, size and materials. If you are installing a particularly large bath, the first questions to consider are whether you have enough water to fill it and whether the floor is strong enough to hold bath, bather and water when full.

Porcelain-enamelled cast iron is still widely favoured as an exceptionally durable material resistant to chemicals and stains, scratches and cracks, and for its substantial feel and heat-insulating properties, as well as its slightly uneven, highly reflective surface. The nature of the material and the manufacturing process mean that cast-iron baths tend to be fairly conventional in shape. The main advantage of the acrylic alternative is that it is much lighter than cast iron, making it easier to install and to increase the size by far more than would be practical in cast iron. It can also be made in a greater variety of shapes than other materials. Reinforced acrylic baths can be substantial in feel and well insulated.

Pressed steel is also lighter than cast iron and usually more economic; it can also be recycled. The manufacturing process means there can be many variations in shape, although this material does not have the heat- and sound-insulating properties of cast iron. Institutional ranges include stainless steel baths, although these can be rather forbidding.

Generally, baths can be either freestanding, panelled, inset or boxed in, allowing for a surround on which to place utensils. Some, like the Morrison (pic 5), come with aprons. Panelled baths tend to be fitted against the wall (see pages 78-79), but this is not necessarily so. In the Langlands and Bell bathroom (see pages 82-85), an enamelled cast-iron bath is positioned centrally and finished with plywood panelling. In the Sporre bathroom (see pages 42-47), a contoured Ideal Standard acrylic bath designed to be boxed in is left exposed with supports visible, so that it appears strangely insectoid.

There are many variations in bath shapes, including asymmetric forms, complex contoured interiors with grips and handles, tubs shaped to combine shower and bath, tubs moulded for two people (see pages 100-3) and tubs with seats and steps, although these can be extraordinarily ugly, especially compared to the satisfying utilitarian form of the conventional bath. Certain ranges such as Ideal Standard's compact Space and Studio are designed for smaller bathrooms and include wider, shorter baths in lengths from 120 cm to 170 cm. Equally, a deep soak tub takes up considerably less floor space than a conventional bath.

Many baths can be ordered with tap holes, or without – for use with wall- or surround-mounted taps and spout, or a freestanding fixture. Double-ended baths have a central waste so that two people can bathe together. In the glass bath (see pages 72-73), the water empties and fills through the waste, so there is no need to have taps or spout distracting from the sculptural form. Vola and Hansgrohe manufacture combined fillers and overflows.

The trend for technologically advanced bathing status symbols took off in the 1970s with the jacuzzi, and now many baths can be orderd in whirlpool and hydromassage or spa versions, which whip up the water with jets of air or massage different parts of the body. These can be taken to extremes with underwater music, light effects and much more.

Besides manufactured baths, there are many possibilities for custom-made tubs, and designers go to inventive lengths to come up with alternative solutions, sometimes rooted in historical precedents such as the Japanese wooden soak tubs or sarcophagus-like carved stone or marble baths. The Japanese wooden soak tub is much deeper and shorter than its western counterpart, and allows the bather to soak up to the chin in a sitting rather than lying position. These wooden baths were originally 172 cm long, 84 cm wide and 56 cm deep, but now they are usually scaled down to fit smaller spaces. Woods are chosen to release a scent when wet – usually Japanese cypress or Chinese black pine, although Japanese cedar and chestnut are also used. In most Japanese homes convenience has overtaken aesthetic considerations and soak tubs made from steel, enamel, tile and the ubiquitious acrylic baths are almost universal, and come in many sizes.

Increasingly, designers are experimenting with alternative shapes and materials for the bath. Glasgow-based Submarine produce giant stainless steel baths that look like a receptacle from a brewery or lab. Claudio Silvestrin's i fiumi range for Boffi includes a round stone bath that sits low on the floor like a giant bowl (pic 7). Carved from a solid block, not surprisingly it is extremely expensive. Generally, the prohibitive cost of carving a large block of stone or marble means that baths are made from slabs of stone reinforced at the corners. John Pawson is currently designing a bathroom range for Obumex which will include a soak tub.

Photographs:
1 Roll-top bath by Jacob Delafon, raised on blocks.
2 Bath designed by Philippe Starck for Hoesch.
3 and 4 Custom-made baths can be finished in many surfaces including plaster and mosaic tiles.
5 Apron bath designed by Jasper Morrison for Bette.
6 Vast stainless steel bath in an apartment by Brookes Stacey Randall.
7 Stone bath in the i fiumi range by Claudio Silvestrin for Boffi.
8 Japanese-style wooden soak tub.

1

2

3

4

The custom-made pool bath has become another popular alternative, favoured for aesthetic considerations as well as for providing more spacious and comfortable dimensions for communal bathing. Such baths can be fabricated and finished in many ways and it is worth seeking specialist advice. In the blue bathroom (see pages 48–51), the bath is constructed on a wooden form lined with fibreglass and plastered. In the bathroom by David Hertz (see pages 76–77), the bath is finished with a slate-coloured waterproof Venetian plaster used for swimming pools. Such baths can be tiled, like Le Corbuisier's sunken rectangular bath for Madame Savoye (see pages 104-5), lined with stone (see pages 106-7) or faced in marble as in the New York penthouse (see pages 58-61) where the surround and steps are generous enough to take books and utensils or make a seat.

Glass is a daring and disconcerting material for bathing,

playing with ideas of weightlessness and introducing a new angle on voyeurism. Masakazu Bokura's bath (see pages 72 and 94–95) is made from tempered glass by master craftsmen.

While conservationists complain about the use of large baths that take lavish quantities of water to fill, it should be noted that in the Japanese household cleansing takes place outside the tub and the same bath water is used by all the family – sometimes bathing communally, sometimes taking it in turns. This may well be less profligate than some western habits.

Showers

The kind of shower you install depends on how and where it will be used. If the basic choice was once a shower over the bath or a shower tray or enclosure, the open shower – where the shower is in a wet room with a drained floor or in part of a room screened off for the purpose – is now a liberating alternative. State-of-the-art showers can resemble space capsules but, as with pretty much everything else in the bathroom, the enduring trend is towards simplification – and a shower need be no more than a shower head set in masonry, a discreet control and a drain in the floor.

An open shower requires careful planning, not least a consideration of what will get wet or how to divide wet and dry areas, and where to keep towels and clothes. While there is nothing nicer than taking a shower with plenty of room to move around, equally there is nothing worse than paddling across a wet floor to use

a mirror or discovering that your towels are soaked.

Drainage is the crucial issue in an open shower or wet room: the floor is effectively a large shower tray, usually slightly sloped to a drain. This can be achieved in different ways, depending on the scale and type of building. Regulations vary from country to country, and waterproofing a floor requires expert advice. In the Los Angeles bathroom (see page 76-77), the blue stone floor slopes to a copper-lined drainage channel along one wall, which is made wide enough for it not to get clogged by stray hairs and bits of soap. In the New York loft bathroom (see page 86-89), the shower is open at one end of the room and the tiled floor slopes gently so that water runs to a central drain, but the lavatory and basin are positioned far enough away to remain dry. In the apartment designed by De Cotiis (see pages 100-3), the overhead shower with body jets is partly contained in an alcove. In the Bath apartment (see

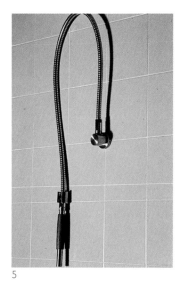

5

6

7

8

pages 98-99), the shower is concealed behind a curved plaster screen, and a custom-made metal drainage tray is set beneath the teak decking, shaped to the space. In the London bathroom (see pages 64-69), water drains through the gaps between the paving stones.

The basis of a successful shower is an adequate flow of water and an even temperature. The first question is whether or not there is enough water and adequate pressure to accommodate the shower, and a specialist should be consulted on the installation. Certain combination boilers, for instance, make 23-25 litres per minute, and some power showers alone can use more than that. In the UK, almost invariably you will need to install a pump to boost the system in order to enjoy a decent shower. Pumps can be fitted for the whole supply to a home, for a bathroom, or just for the shower.

While the shower is generally thought of as an economical option compared to bathing, the reality

depends on the type of shower and for how long it is used. In the UK, metering in new and converted properties has come about partly because of the amount of water used by sprinklers and power showers. Some manufacturers, such as Hansgrohe, make showers with eco-options that reduce consumption.

The other key choice is the type of shower head. One of the most effective overhead shower heads is the deluge, resembling a giant watering-can rose delivering a tropical downpour. Traditional designs are made by Barber Wilson and Czech & Speake, among others. In the loft apartment (see pages 106-7), the adjustable shower head is by Hansgrohe. Many shower heads offer varying force and jet types.

Shower heads can be either fixed into the wall with concealed pipework or mounted on exposed arms, risers or slider bars with flexible hoses so that the head height can be varied. Similarly,

thermostats can be buried in the wall or exposed. Single-control thermostatic valves control the temperature of the water, while with dual thermostatic valves one regulates water flow and the other allows the temperature to be fixed. Showers can also have body jets in imitation of thalassotherapy and other aqua therapies set into the wall or incorporated in a shower enclosure.

Some showers and certain industrial fittings are suitable for use outdoors. On the Paris roof terrace (see pages 122-23), the shower units with exposed piping are by Italian manufacturers Stella. In the Rutherfoord outdoor shower (see page 14), there is a diverter so that you can step directly from the inside shower to warm water outside. Institutional ranges include showers with a water reservoir which do not require plumbing outdoors.

Photographs:

1 Shower head by Stella, on a fixed arm.
2 Ceiling-mounted deluge shower head.
3 Wall-mounted shower head by Vola.
4 Minimal shower head by Boffi.
5 Minimal hand-held shower by Boffi.
6 Shower on a flexible hose, where a scaffold conceals the water supply and acts as a support.
7 Reconditioned shower unit incorporating overhead shower and body sprays.
8 Reconditioned shower unit which mixes hot and cold water in the cylinder.

1

2

3

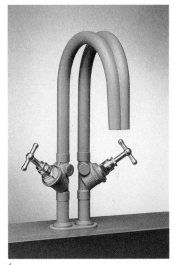

4

Taps and Spouts

There are many different types of
tap available, and your choice should
depend on what you want a tap to
do as well as what it looks like. It is
often forgotten that a tap is as much
about the movement of the water it
delivers and how it is to operate as
about the look of the hardware, and
you should always try to test taps
before making a decision. Some
taps – mostly those in overly
clever designer ranges – turn filling
a bath into an ingenuity test, making
you long for a traditionally
straightforward tap. Different valve
options are available depending on
the purpose, such as a water-saving
mixer for a washbasin or a high-flow
combination for filling a bath. Many
of the more enduring designs are
discreet without being tricksy.

Most continental and American
fittings are designed for a high-
pressure water supply and require
the installation of a pump to work
in the UK, although certain
manufacturers such as Hansgrohe

make low-pressure models for the
British market. However, planners
advise that a pump is preferable
wherever possible. You should
consult a showroom before purchase
to check that the supply is
compatible with the fittings, which
in turn must fit the sanitary ware.

For baths and basins, a basic
choice is whether taps are attached
to the sanitary ware or mounted
separately on the wall or adjacent
counter – a solution allowing greater
freedom in positioning and cleaner
lines. The simplest and cheapest
option for a basin is a pair of pillar
taps which are secured directly into
the basin holes, and it can also have
a pop-up waste. Single (hot and
cold) taps can also be used for baths,
although a mixer tap makes it much
easier to control water temperature
and flow. A three-hole basin mixer
consists of two separate valves which
mix the water before it issues from a
central spout, while a monobloc mixer
requires only a single hole and has
either two controls or a central lever

and mixes the water in the spout.

Baths can be filled using either
a mixer unit fixed on the bath or
mounted on the deck or wall, or two
independent valves and a spout –
a more flexible option that allows
you to position the components as
you wish. Bath mixers can also have
a connection for a shower hose and
a diverter so the water flow can be
directed to the shower. Some also
have a control for the water outlet,
so that bath or basin can be emptied
without the hassle of a plug.

If many designers try to
make taps and spout as discreet
as possible, in the Sheats residence
(see pages 110-15) John Lautner
manages a disappearing act,
concealing the spout behind a mirror,
with water activated by a sensor
when you pass your hand through
a beam. Such systems are
manufactured for commercial use.
For baths, the most discreet option
is a combined bath inlet and waste
or overflow fitting, so that the bath
is filled from within. In the Masakazu

Bokura bathroom (see pages 72-73),
the filler system combining the inlet
with the waste was custom made.
Hansgrohe manufacture Exofill, a
filler fixed in the bath at overflow
height. Vola make a more discreet
fitting which also combines the filler
with the overflow.

Vola has become a designer
hallmark used by architects and
designers all around the world (pic
1). Designed by the Danish architect
Arne Jacobsen in the mid-1960s, the
modular system of valves, handles
and outlets was a response to
manufacturer I.P. Lund's proposal for
a new type of wall-mounted mixer
tap where all parts of the mixer are
hidden, leaving only the handles and
spout visible. Although chrome is the
most common finish, the fittings are
also available in a matt brass (pic 1),
white (see page 96) and various
colours. Boffi's Minimal range (pic 7)
is a recent and similarly low-key
alternative. Philippe Starck's designs
for Axor recall a water-diviner's
forked stick. The taps by Sheardown

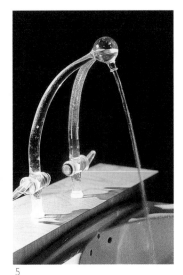

5

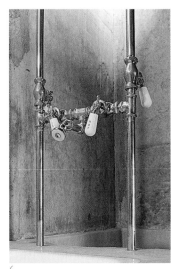

6

7

8

9

10

in the Sporre bathroom (see pages 42-47) look futuristic but are remarkably difficult to use.

The Dutch designer collective Droog bring characteristic imaginative thinking to the tap. In their transparent mixer (pic 5), the water is coloured by light, so that you see the hot red and cold blue water rising in each pipe and mixing in the spout. Another Droog design with hose-like spouts (pic 4) looks as though it has been abducted from the laboratory.

Industrial manufacturers are a good source for reasonably priced hardware widely exploited by designers and architects. Many industrial taps are made for particular purposes such as hospital, catering and institutional uses, but can equally well be applied to the domestic bathroom. As well as lever taps that can be turned on and off with a flick of the elbow, there are numerous other variations, including foot pedals. In the Young apartment (see pages 124-27), the taps are

manufactured by Toni Armatur. Equally, standard brass outdoor taps (pic 9), the Deux Chevaux of taps, are handsome and utilitarian budget fittings.

Some salvage merchants and reclamation yards specialize in old and reconditioned bathroom hardware as well as sanitary ware. The appeal is usually the scale and solidity of the fittings as opposed to more discreet modern styles. Both the Parr bathroom (pic 2, and see pages 86-89) and the New York loft (see pages 54-57) use old fittings. You should always check first that such fittings are compatible with your sanitary ware and water supply, or whether they can be adapted. Some manufacturers, including Czech & Speake and Barber Wilson in the UK, Urban Archaeology in the United States and Stella in Italy (see page 122), make traditional fittings with solidity rather than simply glitz.

The celebration of water can be a defining feature of bathroom design, and to exploit this potential

some architects and designers have spouts custom-made to their own design. A hallmark of John Pawson's and Claudio Silvestrin's bathrooms is the sculptural swan-neck spout – an elegant arc accentuated by the stream of water. In the Langlands and Bell bathroom (see pages 82-83), the bath taps and spout were made by a plumber.

Photographs:
1 Brass wall-mounted taps and
spout by Vola.
2 The tap is part of a reconditioned
shower unit in the Parr bathroom.
3 Institutional ranges are a good source
of bathroom hardware.
4 Taps by Droog, modelled on lab fittings.
5 In Droog's transparent tap you can see
the hot red and cold blue water rising in
the pipes and mixing.
6 Schindler incorporated taps controlling
bath and basin in his 'plumbing tree'.
7 Shower control from Boffi's
Minimal range.
8 Tara by Dornbracht.
9 Outdoor brass taps make basic controls
in a shower.
10 Shower control by Kroin.

Mirrors

The mirror is considered more or less essential to the bathroom – at least in the west – although how mirrors are used rather depends on whether you enjoy reflections or find them disturbing. Where the 1970s went mad mirroring great expanses of wall, so that bathrooms made you feel as if you were in a shop or had checked into a hotel, more recently designers have tended to use mirrors in as low-key and discreet a way as possible.

The minimum is usually at least a mirror beside a washbasin, to be used for shaving, making-up and so on. Mirrors can be incorporated into a medicine cabinet, as in the Mizrahi bathroom (see pages 78-79), where the mirror conceals storage with open shelves beside it, or into other forms of storage as in the London loft apartment (see pages106-7), where the mirror panel in the wall flaps open to reveal a cupboard. Or, you can simply set a panel of mirror flush against the wall (pic 2).

Depending on materials and manufacture, mirrors have different qualities and tints, such as appearing warm or cool, and if you buy directly from a glass supplier you should be able to choose from a considerable range. Electric heating pads applied to the rear of a mirror prevent it steaming up with condensation, which is particularly important in enclosed bathrooms.

A basin mirror can be no more than the size of a shaving mirror – mounted on a flexible arm, it can be adjusted to the light source,

obviating the need to install a light beside the mirror. In the Manhattan loft (see pages 48-51; pic 4), the mirror is not only on an adjustable arm but is fixed on a suction pads, so that it can be moved around the room. The oval vertical mirrors are also adjustable and can be used as a playful sculptural addition to lighten the architecture, in a way that is reminiscent of a Calder mobile.

Alternatives to conventional mirrors can be found in industrial catalogues. In the Los Angeles shower room (see pages 74-75), Brian Murphy has hung a convex mirror, of the sort used on roads and in shops, on the back of a door, throwing the room into a surreal dimension. These can be sourced from industrial glass and mirror manufacturers. In another cloakroom (see pages 80-81), Murphy uses giant truck wing mirrors which are conveniently adjustable.

Depending on the function of the room – if, for instance, the bathroom doubles as a dressing room – it may need larger mirrors. In the Sporre house (see page 42-47), the carved gilt mirror brings a sense of femininity to the bathroom, and as it is propped against the wall, slightly tilted, the effect is not quite as disconcerting as walking into a room to find a full-length image of oneself directly ahead. In the Italian apartment (pic 1), the freestanding wall behind the basin is covered with highly polished stainless steel, which gives a slightly softer reflection than glass mirrors.

1

2

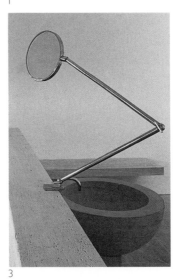

3

4

5

6

Lighting

As water and electricity are a potentially dangerous, if not fatal, combination, lighting needs to be addressed with particular care in the bathroom. Regulations concerning the installation of electrics and light fittings vary and you should consult a qualified electrician. In the UK, where rules governing the use of electricity in bathrooms are strict, electric sockets are banned from bathroom use apart from specially insulated shaver sockets; light fittings must be steamproof; lights must be operated either by a cord or by a switch outside the bathroom, and so on. Yet safety factors aside, the importance of lighting in establishing the mood of a bathroom, as of any other room, is often underrated. Often, it is caught in the tug-of-war between practicality and pleasure – although there is is no reason why the two cannot be combined.

The best light source for the bathroom is, of course, direct natural light. Even in an internal bathroom natural light can be let in by inserting a glass wall or panel, or skylight.

Bathrooms without windows or a natural light source require special attention. Certain activities, such as shaving or making-up, require careful lighting, there is nothing less conducive to rest than a bathroom that is as brightly lit as a surgery. However, take into account such activities as reading in the bath. Fitting dimmer switches makes it possible to change the mood.

Conventional bathroom lighting schemes combine ceiling or wall lights for background lighting with some sort of task light beside the washbasin and mirror. Standard solutions are a strip light over the mirror or one on either side, or low-wattage bulbs ranked at the side. But fluorescent tubes can be concealed behind mirrors, creating a halo of light around the edge.

The choice of bathroom light fittings is surprisingly restricted. Industrial sourcebooks are a good hunting ground, especially for marine lighting (pic 3) and fittings intended for use outdoors.

In the Japanese bath house and the sauna, lighting is kept low so as not to chase away the steamy shadows. The sauna is traditionally illuminated by an oil lamp or candle. Candlelight can, of course, be ideal in the bathroom. In the Sporre bathroom (see pages 42-45), candles are mounted on the tall mirror, maximizing the light – in fact, mirrors can be positioned to enhance all sorts of light sourcesand schemes.

The hamam interior is characterized by the dramatic manipulation of daylight, using small windows studding the dome to cast intense shafts of light, an idea recalled in modern form in the Soft and Hairy House by Ushida Findlay (see page 37). Equally, natural light from windows can be manipulated in different ways. In the futuristic Italian apartment (see pages 100-2), the shutter over the large circular window has horizontal slits that allow in slots of light – and ventilation.

1

2

3

4

Lavatories

The lavatory is the most complex of the bathroom fittings and the slowest to change, because new designs have to be tested to fulfil different requirements in different markets. Sanitation systems differ from country to country and you should always check with the supplier that a design is suitable or can be adapted. The lavatory is also usually the least flexible component to site, as positioning may be dictated by the soil stack.

Many versions of the WC exist, with different flushing systems and in an enormous range of styles. Which you choose depends partly on whether there is space to conceal the cistern or not. With high-level lavatories the pan and cistern are separated by a flush pipe, and these tend to be traditional in design. Close-coupled WCs have the cistern and pan attached. Back-to-wall pans have a separate plastic cistern concealed behind a false wall or ceiling and can be wall hung or floor mounted. Usually there is a minimum height at which the cistern must be installed to flush correctly and a specialist should be consulted.

Often, designers try to conceal the lavatory. In the John Pawson bathroom (see pages 64-69), it is hidden in a stone bench rather like an old-fashioned wooden water closet. In the Langlands and Bell bathroom (see pages 84-85), it is built into an alcove.

Designs should be chosen for comfort as well as looks. Ranges such as Ideal Standard's Space, designed for compact spaces, include variations such as corner WCs and seats which can be turned at 45 degrees to right or left to suit a particular room. Certain designs – such as Space, and Starck's lavatory for Duravit which is modelled on a generic pail – may not suit larger people. Some institutional ranges have stainless steel lavatories and for prisons, there are models without a seat or rim (pic 1).

Height is another aspect to consider. The standard lavatory measures 400–410 cm from floor to seat. Wall-hung lavatories can be fixed at varied heights and for many people, especially the less agile, a higher seat is more comfortable.

Noise varies depending on the type of flush and how the cistern works. On the whole, syphonic lavatories are quieter than washdown. It is especially worth thinking about noise in situations where a lavatory is close to the bedroom and likely to wake a partner in the middle of the night.

The flush itself can be either part of the lavatory or separate, the latter usually in wall-hung WCs. Geberit produce a concealed cistern with a push-panel flush (see pages 42-47). In terms of invisibilility, one neat solution made for commercial washrooms is the remote beam/sensor through which you pass your hand to activate the flush.

With seats, the choice is not only in the materials – wood, various plastics and so on – but also in how the hinge mechanism works. Pressalit, among others, manufacture a seat with a hydraulic hinge, so that instead of clashing it floats gently down. In Japan, where bathrooms often don't have central heating, the heated lavatory seat is a popular innovation.

In many countries the flush is now down to 6 litres or less. Waterless flushes, similar to the systems used on airplanes and in some hotels, are available but they have yet to take off outside the commercial market.

Photographs:
1 Stainless steel lavatory designed for prison use.
2 Lavatory set in an alcove and angled to provide leg room.
3 A freestanding WC with exposed pipes becomes a sculptural form.
4 Wall-hung lavatory with a concealed cistern.

1

2

3

4

Bidets

Whether or not a bidet is included in the bathroom is a cultural issue – and also a matter of space. While bidets are standard fittings in continental Europe, they remain a rarity in the United States.

As with lavatories, bidets can be floor mounted or wall hung, supported on brackets hidden behind a false wall which also conceals the plumbing. Usually, they are selected to match the WC and are also ceramic. In the John Young apartment (see pages 124-27), a stainless steel institutional lavatory has been adapted to become a bidet. Bidets usually have a single hole and take a bidet tap. Again, wall-hung versions can be varied in height. In Japan, Toto manufacture combined lavatory/bidets with a dazzling array of washing and drying controls, and have launched a simplified version for the American market.

Heating

Warmth is fundamental to making a bathroom an inviting place in which to undress. How warm, though, is a personal issue. In colder climates, the bathroom may be kept considerably warmer than other rooms in the home. In one London house, for instance, the architects fitted a sliding glass door separating bathroom from bedroom, so that the bathroom could be kept at 24°C and the bedroom cooler.

Underfloor heating was used by the Romans to heat their baths and adopted in the hamam.

Recent technologies have made it increasingly easy to install underfloor heating in the home. Besides the pleasure of an even heat and warm floor surface, concealed systems are the least obtrusive designwise. They are particularly suitable for the bathroom, where you are likely to spend a lot of time barefoot, and especially for materials such as stone, tiles or concrete, which can be chilly underfoot. Equally, certain systems can also be fitted in the wall or ceiling.

While systems using hot water require a certain depth to accommodate the pipes or hose, electric mat systems are especially easy to install for one room such as the bathroom and can be so slim that they only add 5 mm to the depth of the floor. As underfloor heating operates at low temperatures, it is suitable for many floor finishes, including wood, without any fear of scorching or warping. Systems such as Thermofloor come in different strengths, so that they can be used just to take the chill out of the floor or actually to heat the room. The thermostat can be programmed to keep the floor at the temperature you like to walk on, regardless of variations in the room. Such systems are used for marble baths to keep steps warm and even to warm the bath itself.

In the Young apartment (see pages 124-27), the concrete is heated underfloor and assisted by an industrial fin radiator wrapping around the room beside the supply pipes. Skirting systems have the advantage over radiators that they are usually more discreet and emit heat evenly all around the room. Hot pipes left exposed can also assist in heating a bathroom.

Heated towel rails, and towel rails extended to make ladder or panel radiators, can either be linked into the central heating system or electricity, or a combination, so that you can have warm, dry towels even when the central heating is turned off.

Steam and sauna

The sauna and steam room are generally the most easily domesticated forms of steam bath, and are not necessarily that expensive to install compared to, say, a complex hydromassage tub. Which you choose depends partly on whether you prefer the dry heat of the sauna or the much more humid steam bath. A sauna usually operates at 80–100°C with humidity as low as 3 per cent RH, while a steam bath runs at 40–42°C with humidity around 100 per cent RH.

A shower room can be built to be watertight and double as a steam room, or some shower cubicles can be converted if they can be sealed. Acrylic domes are made to fit over shower cubicles. Alternatively, manufacturers such as Nordic make steam/shower cubicles and cabins. The disadvantage with ready-made cabins is that they tend to be moulded plastic capsules, and designwise it is usually preferable to custom-build.

Once a room is watertight, all it really requires is a steam generator such as Multi steam, which is fitted outside the room, and all that is visible inside is the control panel which monitors temperature and a discreet steam nozzle. The size of the generator depends on the dimensions of the room, and a specialist should advise this. Seating preferably consists of a bench or tiered benches long enough to lie down on.

Saunas can also be bought as ready-made cabins, or custom-built with specialist advice. Essentially, a sauna is simply a well-insulated room lined with a wood with a low resin content, such as spruce, and heated by a stove. Wood should never be treated, as this contaminates the steam. Correct ventilation is essential for comfort and operation. Swedish manufacturers such as Tylö supply ready-made cabins and electric and wood-burning stoves, as well as making cabins to architects' specifications.

GREAT BATHING EXPERIENCES

Many of the joys of bathing are to be found far from the domestic bathroom or even the increasing numbers of spas promoting water therapies. This is a partial and brief guide to a few extraordinary bathing places encountered in the process of researching this book.

ENGLAND

The Porchester Spa
Porchester Road
Queensway
London W2
Tel: 0171 792 3980

Despite the turn-of-the-century fashion for Turkish baths, unfortunately there are few survivors. The stern grandeur of the era is recalled in the palatial warm room upstairs in Porchester Baths. Then you descend via the chilling plunge pool into the bowels of the building to more utilitarian tiled hot rooms and steam rooms. Although fairly recently restored, the spa still has a slightly dowdy municipal tang.

FINLAND

Sauna-Seera
Lauttasaari
Tel: 00 358 9 67 86 77

Lauttasaari, an island south of Helsinki in the Gulf of Finland, is home to the Finnish sauna society, who still run traditional smoke saunas. In this method, favoured by sauna aficionados, the smoke from the khios stove is kept in the room until just before the bathers enter, so they are immersed in the thick heat of the dark, smoke-stained timber buildings. In between sessions you can cool off in the Gulf of Finland.

FRANCE

Hammam de la Mosquee
Place du Puits-de-l'Ermite
Paris 75005
Tel: 00 33143313820

Along with couscous and rai music, the hamam was adopted by the French as a result of their colonial associations with North Africa and the Islamic world. Built in the 1920s and recently restored, the ornate hamam and tea rooms are part of the Hispano-Moorish style tiled mosque compound.

ITALY

Terme di Saturnia
Grossetto
Tel: 00 3905 644 60 10 61

Tuscany's hills are riddled with miles of thermal streams, waterfalls and limestone pools originating from underwater sulphur springs. As well as endearingly old-fashioned spas like those at Saturnia where Italians still go to 'take the waters', there are informal bathing places where people scramble up the hillside to dip into the warm pools. At night the scene has laws of its own – especially on the full moon. The communal spring-water bath, built entirely of stone like an open-air living room, is well worth a visit.

JAPAN

Azumaya Inn
Yunomine
Hongu-machi
Wakayama-ken
Tel: 00 81 735 420 012

There are several thousand hot springs onsen resorts in Japan, and numerous guide books extolling different locations and the benefits of the waters. At Yunomine, high in the mountains of Wakayama province, the small isolated village is submerged in steam rising from the hot springs which bubble up beside the river. According to legend, a mortally wounded samurai was brought back to life by bathing in the waters. You can still bathe in the same rock bath housed in a shed clamped to the river's edge (pages 20-21). Water spouts out at over 60°C and the bather lies embalmed in a mildly sulphurous fug, watching the cold river race by. The Azumaya Inn is a modest rustic onsen inn with a magnificent bath house clad in dark wood.

SWEDEN

Hasseluden Konferens & Yasuragi
132 81 Saltsjo-Boo
Stockholm
Tel: 00 468 747 6100

There is a strong empathy between Scandiniavian and Japanese design – the love of natural materials, simple forms and respect for wood craftsmanship – and the Hasseluden is an example of what can happen when the two cultures cross. This is a health resort outside Stockholm in a rudimentary 1970s concrete building, recently renovated by Franz Hardinger, containing hot springs, baths, eastern design references, and a pool building lined and decked in wood. With wood deeply rooted in the bathing cultures of both Scandinavia and Japan, it is interesting to see it used again for bathing and contemporary interpretations of traditions.

SWITZERLAND

Thermal Baths
Hotel Therme
7132 Vals
Tel: 0041 819 26 80 80

The Thermal Baths, designed by architect Peter Zumthor, offer an exciting addition to the great traditions of balneary architecture and have instantly become a site for cult architectural pilgrimage. In Zumthor's monolithic and rigorously minimalist design, the combination of water, light and striated grey stone left with the roughness of rock transcends the physical and recalls ancient bathing places.

TURKEY

Istanbul

Once known as the steam capital of the world, Istanbul's hamams have been sinking into dilapidation for decades, but it is still the place to enjoy this remnant of the Ottoman age. The survivors are either monuments such as the hamam in Cağaloğlu, or else those in populous districts of the city where there is still call for public bath houses. The Cağaloğlu hamam, built in 1741 by Mahmut I, is famous for its Ottoman-style cruciform steam room with windowed dome supported on a circle of columns and ornately baroque taps and marble basins.

SUPPLIERS

MATERIALS AND FINISHES

Armourcoat
Morewood Close
London Road
Sevenoaks
Kent TN13 2HU
t 01723 460668
f 01732 450930
www.armourcoat.co.uk
Coloured and polished hard plasters.

Blu
The Barn
Pilmore Lane
Watchfield
Somerset TA9 4LB
t 01278 793644
f 01278 787865
www.blu-uk.com
*Blu manufacture a multi-purpose
glass product 'Igo' that can be used
to clad entire bathrooms (walls and
floors) and can be coloured with
pigments and combined with
fibre-optics for striking effects.
Also launching a polished steel
bath and an egg-shaped glass bath.*

Granite and Marble International
Westminster House
Pensbury Place
Wandsworth Road
London SW8 4TD

t 0171 498 2742
f 0171 498 0384
*Supply and fit granite and
marble and other natural stones.*

Luxcrete Ltd
Premier House
Disraeli Road
Park Royal
London NW10 7BT
t 0181 965 7292
f 0181 961 6337
*Luxcrete glass bricks and Italian
and German glass bricks.*

Pilkington UK Ltd
Prescot Road
St Helen's
Merseyside WA10 3TT
t 01744 692000
*Glass manufacturers, who also make
innovative structural glazing systems.*

Preedy Glass
Lamb Works
North Road
London N7 9DP
t 0171 700 0377
f 0171 700 7579
Wide range of glass, mirrors etc.

Reed Harris
Riverside House
27 Carnwath Road
London SW6 3HR
t 0171 736 7511
f 0171 736 2988
*Mosaic tiles and marble stone
and slate tiles for walls and floors.*

Solarglass
Herald Way
Binley
Coventry CV3 2ND
t 01203 458844
f 01203 547777
*Division of French glass
manufacturers Saint Gobains
who supply architectural glasses
including Privalite, the electrically
operated glass that changes from
transluscent to clear when you
pass a current through it.*

Stone Age
19 Filmer Road
London SW6 7BU
t 0171 385 7954/5
f 0171 385 7956
www.info@stone-age.co.uk
*Specialists in limestone
and sandstone.*

Syndesis
2908 Colorado Avenue
Santa Monica
California 90404
USA
t 00 1 310 829 9932
f 00 1 310 829 5641
*Manufacturers of Syndecrete, a
lightweight cement-based surfacing
material used for bath tubs, sinks etc.*

Udny, Edgar & Co
314 Balham High Road
London SW17 7AA
t 0181 767 8181
f 0181 767 7709
*Mosaic tiles including Bisazza's
Vetricolor Venetian glass tiles, and
ceramic and vitrified mosaic tiles.*

Vermont Soapstone Co
PO Box 268
248 Stoughton Pond Road
Perkinsville
VT 05151 0268
USA
t 00 1 802 263 5404
f 00 1 802 263 9451
www.vermont.soapstone.com
*Basins and tubs made to measure
in vermont soapstone.*

FITTINGS

Alternative Plans
9 Hester Road
London SW11 4AN
t 0171 228 6460
f 0171 924 1164
Showroom and suppliers for
Boffi, Agape, Nito, Rapsel, Santini.

Associated Metal (Stainless) Ltd
101 Brook Street
Glasgow G40 3AP
t 0141 551 0707
f 0141 551 0690
www.assoc-metal.co.uk
Manufacture stainless steel baths,
basins, w.c.s, shower trays and
cubicles etc.

GEC Anderson Ltd
Oakengrove
Shire Lane
Hastoe
Hertfordshire HP23 6LY
t 01442 826999
f 01442 825999
Stainless steel lavatories, basins,
washing troughs designed for
institutional use.

Aston-Matthews
141-147 Essex Road
Islington
London N1 2FN
t 0171 226 7220
f 0171 354 5951
Bathroom showroom with large
range of cast iron baths and
stockists for Barber Wilson taps
and showers.

Axor (see Hansgrohe below)
Division of Hansgrohe who produce
a range of taps by Starck that
compliment his lines for Duravit
and Hoesch.

Badekabiner
Spettrupvej 123
8722 Hedensted
Denmark
t 00 45 7589 2400
f 00 45 7589 1824
Danish manufacturers of pre-
fabricated bathroom pods used
in hotels and student hostels and
housing development including
Montevetro where the prefabricated
units have glass basins.

Barber Wilson
Crawley Road
Westbury Avenue
Wood Green
London N22 6AH
t 0181 888 3461
f 0181 888 2041
Manufacture taps, showerheads etc.

The Bathroom
Showroom Association
Federation House
Station Road
Stoke-on-Trent
Staffordshire ST4 2SA
t 01782 844006
f 01782 844614
Trade organisation that can
advise on bathroom manufacturers
and suppliers.

Bette UK
Park View
Lower Clopton
Upper Quinton
Stratford-upon-Avon
Warwickshire CV37 8LQ
t 01386 438315
f 01386 438046
Bath manufacturers including
the Morrison by Jasper Morrison.

Boffi Bagni
Via Oberdan, 70
20030 Lentate sul Seveso
Milan
Italy
t 00 39 0362 5341
f 00 39 0362 565077
UK: Alternative Plans as above.
Washbasins, bathroom furniture
and accessories by Piero Lissoni,
Marc Sadler, Claudio Silvestrin's
i Fiumi stone baths and basins etc.

Boffi Solferino
Via Solferino
20121 Milan
Italy
t 00 39 0289 13217
Elegant showroom for
Boffi Bagni products.

Czech & Speake Showroom
39c Jermyn Street
London SW1Y 6DN
t 0171 439 0216
Head office:
244-254 Cambridge Heath Road
London E2 9DA

Direct Shop
(Czech & Speake mail order)
UK mail order:
freephone 0800 919728
international mail order:
t 00 44 181 980 4567
Period bathroom fittings including
large shower heads.

Dornbracht
Unit 3 Oakwood Industrial Park
Gatwick Road
Crawley
West Sussex RH10 2AZ
www.dornbracht.com
e info@dornbracht.de
t 01293 531313
f 01293 531310
UK: Splash
German manufacturers of taps and
plumbing equipment including Tara
(page 145).

Droog
DMD, Parkweg 14
2271 AJ Voorburg
Holland
t 00 31 70 386 4038
f 00 31 70 387 3075
Experimental designers whose
bathroom products include
functional tiles (page 133), taps
(page 144-5) and squashy
resin washbasins.

Duravit
Werderstraße 36
Postfach 240
D-78123 Hornberg
Germany
t 00 49 78 33 70 0
f 00 49 78 33 70 289
www.duravit.com
UK: C.P. Hart see below
Washbasins, lavatories and
accessories including ranges
by Philippe Starck.

Elegant John
Unit 6-7
Glenview Industrial Estate
Herberton Road
Rialto
Dublin 12
Eire
t 00 353 1 454 1384
f 00 353 1 454 4220
Showroom stocking Duravit,
Cesame sanitaryware, C.P. Hart
lines among others.

Future Enterprises
290 Ashley Down Road
Bristol BS7 9BQ
t 0117 944 2962
f 0117 924 7347
Omni deep soaking bathtub;
Japanese style tubs in acrylic.

Geberit Terrain
Aylesford
Kent ME20 7PJ
t 01622 717811
f 01622 716920

Manufacturers of flushing lavatory
cisterns including the flushing plate
in the bathroom (pages 44-5).

Hansgrohe
Units D1 & D2
Sandown Park Trading Estate
Royal Mills
Esher
Surrey KT10 8BL
t 01372 465655
f 01372 470670
www.hansgrohe.co.uk
German manufacturers of taps,
shower fittings etc.

C.P. Hart
Newnham Terrace
Hercules Road
London SE1 7DR
t 0171 902 1000
f 0171 902 1001
As well as own ranges of ceramics,
taps, accessories, stockists for
Duravit, Hansgrohe, Vola, Hoesch,
Bette, Multi Steam etc.

Hoesch Metall
Postfach 10 04 24
D-52304 Düren
Germany
t 00 49 24 22 54 0
f 00 49 24 22 67 93
www.hoesch.de
UK: C.P. Hart see above
Baths including designs by
Philippe Starck.

Ideal-Standard
The Bathroom Works
National Avenue
Kingston-upon-Hull
East Riding
Yorkshire HU5 4HS
t 01482 346461
f 01482 445886
www.ideal-standard.co.uk
Collections include Space and
Studio designed for small spaces.

Jacob Delafon
Unit 1, Churchward
Southmead Park
Didcot
Oxfordshire OX11 7HB
t 01235 510511
f 01235 510481
Classic cast iron baths.

LASSCO
Brittannia Walk
London N1 7LU
t 0171 336 8221
f 0171 336 8224
Architectural salvage company; have
a section specialising in reclaimed
bathroom fittings and radiators,
mainly British and French.

Nito
Nitoarredamenti srl
Via E. Mattei 19
53041 Asciano
Siena
Italy
t 00 39 0577 71 8899
f 00 39 0577 71 8733

UK: Alternative Plans see above
Basins and accessories including
washbasin 'morgans' by Andrée
Putman (page 138-139).

Obumex
Diksmuidestraat 121
8840 Staden
Belgium
t 00 32 51 70 50 71
f 00 32 51 70 50 81
Manufacturers of Wash by Vincent
van Duysen (page 138-9).
Also have a line by John Pawson
in development.

Original Bathrooms Ltd
143-145 Kew Road
Richmond-upon-Thames
Surrey TW9 2PN
t 0181 940 7554
f 0181 948 8200
Showroom with baths by Hoesch,
basins by Sicart and Agape etc.

Presalit Ltd
Riverside Business Park
Leeds Road
Ilkley
West Yorkshire LS29 8JZ
t 01943 607651
f 01943 607214
Lavatory seats and products for
the elderly and disabled.

Rapsel
Via Volta, 13
20019 Settimo Milanese
(Mi) Italy

t 00 39 02 33 55 981
f 00 30 02 33 55 1306
*Basins and accessories including
designs by Philippe Starck, Andrée
Putman and Matteo Thun.*

Sheardown Engineering Ltd
15-17 South Road
Templefields
Harlow
Essex CM20 2AP
t 01279 421788
f 01279 435642
*Futuristic-looking Admix taps
designed in the 1970s as used in
Sporre bathroom (pages 44-45) and
also lever taps for hospital use etc.*

W&G Sissons Ltd
Carrwood Road
Chesterfield Trading Estate
Sheepsbridge
Chesterfield S41 9QB
t 01246 450255
f 01246 451276
*Stainless steel sanitaryware.
Will make special orders.*

Submarine
Ushida Findlay Building
1/1, 8 Lanark Street
Glasgow
Scotland G1 5PY
t/f 0141 243 2424
*Handmade stainless steel baths,
including elliptical freestanding Ursulà
tub. Baths can be made to order to
customer's dimensions, also stainless
steel lavatory cisterns and basins.*

Urban Archaeology Company
143 Franklin Street
New York
NY 10013
USA
t 00 1 212 431 4646
f 00 1 212 343 9312
*Original and reproduction American
bathroom fixtures and fittings
including baths, basins, lighting etc.*

Vola UK Ltd
Unit 12
Ampthill Business Park
Station Road
Ampthill
Bedfordshire MK45 2QW
t 01525 841155
f 01525 841177
*Vola range of mixers, showers
and accessories designed by
Arne Jacobsen.*

The Water Monopoly
16/18 Lonsdale Road
London NW6 6RD
t 0171 624 2636
f 0171 624 2631
*Salvaged and restored English and
French fittings mainly from the turn
of the century.*

Waterworks
475 Broome Street
New York
NY 10013
USA
t 00 1 212 274 8800
f 00 1 212 274 0788
*Chain of bathroom showrooms
with modern and more classic
ranges including wash bowls
(see pages 80-81).*

The Yard
32 Montgomery Road
Belfast BT6 9HL
t 01232 405600
f 01232 403908
*Modern bathroom showroom
stocking Duravit, Agape, Nito etc.*

ACCESSORIES

Aram designs
3 Kean Street
London WC2 B4AT
t 0171 240 3933
f 0171 240 3697
*Modern furniture showroom and
stockists of Eileen Gray's Castellar
mirror and light (see pages 126-7).*

Johanna Gullischen
74 rue du Cherche-Midi
75006 Paris
France
t/f 00 33 1 42 22 12 67
*Finnish linen towels for use
after sauna.*

Liwan
8 Rue Saint-Sulpice
75006 Paris
France
t 00 33 1 43 26 07 40
f 00 33 1 40 46 05 71
*Hamam accessories including gloves
and towels, silver bowls, soaps etc.*

Tylö (see below)
*Wooden Sauna equipment, bowls,
ladles etc. see below.*

LIGHTING

Agape (see above)

Catalytico
1-3 Leonard Street
London EC2A 4AQ
t 0171 608 3033
f 0171 608 1688
*Lighting showroom; supply Luceplan's
Metropolis bathroom fittings.*

Davey Lighting
1 Chelmsford Road
Industrial Estate
Great Dunmow
Essex CM6 1HD
t 01371 873174
f 01371 873202
*Large range of lighting for ships
suitable for bathroom use.*

Flos
31 Lisson Grove
London NW1 6UB
t 0171 258 0600
f 0171 723 7005
*Distribute Flos lights including
Bagno light mirror range designed
by Rodolfo Dordoni.*

London Lighting
135 Fulham Road
London SW3 6RT
t 0171 589 3612
f 0171 581 9652
*Modern lighting showroom with
own lines and stockists for Fontana.*

Louis Poulson
Surrey Business Park
Weston Road
Epsom
Surrey KT17 1JG
t 01372 848800
f 01372 848814
*Danish lighting manufacturers with
fittings suitable for bathroom use.*

HEATING

Bisque Radiators
15 Kingsmead Square
Bath
Avon BA1 2AE
t 01225 469244
f 01225 444708
*Modern and classic radiators
and heated towel rails.*

DK Heating
Marlborough House
159 High Road
Wealdstone
Middlesex HA3 5DX
t 0181 861 2844
f 0181 861 2414
www.DKHeating.com
*Supply and install Thermofloor
electric underfloor heating. See
website for international suppliers.*

Thermoboard
Wilmington Building Products
Unit 4, Fairoaks Close
Exeter Airport Business Park
Exeter
Devon EX5 2UL
t 01392 444122
f 01392 444135
*Manufacture underfloor heating
products based on hot water
systems, including Thermoboard,
a modular system incorporating
water pipes in boards. Certain
products are suitable for use
on walls as well as floors.*

STEAM AND SAUNA

Tylö
Svarvaregatan 6
Se-30850
Halmstad
Sweden
t 00 46 35 100080
f 00 46 35 102580

MultiSteam
see C.P. Hart and Tylö
*Steam generators and controls
for domestic steam rooms.*

Nordic
Fairview Estate
Holland Road
Oxted
Surrey RH8 9BZ
f 01883 716970
*Manufacturers of steam rooms,
steam showers, saunas cabins,
heaters and accessories.*

Sauna UK Ltd
Gratton Way
Roundswell Industrial Estate
Barnstaple
Devon EX31 3NL
t 01271 371676
f 01271 371699
*Sauna heaters and cabins etc. Will
build saunas to architects designs.
Also wooden sauna accessories
including buckets, ladles etc.*

ARCHITECTS AND DESIGNERS

Contact details for architects and designers whose work is featured in the main part of the book are included with permission of the architects and designers. While architects and designers are happy to discuss commissions, they do not generally appreciate being contacted for the 'phone number of a tap manufacturer and so on, and where possible these have been included in the suppliers directory.

Ross Anderson
Anderson Architects plc
55 Vandam Street (13th Floor)
New York
NY 10013
USA
t 00 1 212 620 0996
f 00 1 212 620 5299

Masakazu Bokura
B2 Bokura Barbot
108 Rue de la Croix Nivert
75015 Paris
France
t 33 1 42 50 46 46
f 33 1 42 50 56 26

Vincenzo De Cotiis
Via Diaz 18
25100 Brescia
Italy
t 00 39 030 293 225

Jeff Delsalle
7 Rue Seguier
75006 Paris
France
t 00 33 1 432942 76
f 00 33 1 296621

Winka Dubbeldam
Archi-tectonics
111 Mercer Street (2nd floor)
New York
NY 10012
USA
t 00 1 212 226 0303
f 00 1 212 219 3106

Mark Guard Architects
161 Whitfield Street
London W1P 5RY
t 0171 380 1199
f 0171 387 5441

David Hertz
Syndesis
2908 Colorado Avenue
Santa Monica
California 90404
USA
t 00 1 310 829 9932
f 00 1 310 829 5641

Ashley Hicks
Allegra Hicks Design
The Old Imperial Laundry
71 Warriner Gardens (gate 2)
London SW11 4XW
t 0171 720 3669
f 0171 720 2117

John Pawson
Unit B, 70-78 York Way
London N1 9AG
t 0171 837 2929
f 0171 837 4949

Briffa Phillips
19-21 Holywell Hill
St Albans AL1 1EZ
t 01727 840567
f 01727 853325

Royal Institute of British Architects
Clients Advisory Service
66 Portland Place
London W1N 4AD
t 0171 307 3700
f 0171 436 9112
The RIBA run a Clients Advisory Service which advises clients on suitable architects for a particular job.

AUSTRALIAN SUPPLIERS

All Class Bathroom Renovations
9 Delvor Place
Glenhaven
Sydney
t 00 61 2 9894 6044

Bathroom Affair
66 Moss Street
Slacks Creek
Brisbane
t 00 61 07 3841 3366

Bathroom Concepts
169 O'Connell Street
North Adelaide
Adelaide
t 00 61 8 8239 0199

Boucher Jones and Co Pty Ltd
158 Edward Street
Perth
t 00 61 3 9328 6955

Boucher Jones and Co Pty Ltd
587-593 Church Street
Richmond
Melbourne
t 00 61 3 9429 8888

Professional Bathroom Renovations
23 Franklin Street
Lindisfarne
Hobart
t 00 61 3 6243 0066

INDEX

First published in 1999 by
Quadrille Publishing Limited
Alhambra House
27-31 Charing Cross Road
London WC2H OLS

Text © Jane Withers 1999
Special photography © Christoph Kicherer
Design and layouts © Quadrille Publishing Ltd

Publishing Director **Anne Furniss**
Creative Director **Mary Evans**
Consultant Art Director **Helen Lewis**
Design Assistant **Jim Smith**
Picture Research **Nadine Bazar**
Editorial Assistant **Caroline Perkins**
Production **Vincent Smith, Julie Hadingham**

British Library Cataloguing in Publication Data
A catalogue record for this book is available from
the British Library

The moral rights of the Author have been asserted

ISBN 1 902757 01 7

Printed and bound in Hong Kong

BIBLIOGRAPHY

Baths and Bathing in Classical Antiquity by Fikret Yegul
(The Architectural Foundation and The MIT Press,
Cambridge Massachussets and London, England, 1992)

*Clean and Decent, The Fascinating History of the Bathroom
and the WC* by Lawrence Wright
(Routledge & Kegan Paul, London, 1960)

Undesigning the Bath by Leonard Koren
(Stone Bridge Press, Berkeley, California, 1996)

The Bathroom by A. Kira
(Penguin Books, USA, 1974)

Home: A Short History of an Idea by Witold Rybczynski
(Viking Penguin Inc, USA, 1986)

Japan's Hidden Hot Springs by Robert Neff
(Charles E. Tuttle Company, Rutland, Vermont and Tokyo, Japan, 1995)

Geography of Home by Akiko Busch
(Princeton Architectural Press, USA, 1999)

Pleasures of the Japanese Bath by Peter Grilli and
Dana Levy (Weatherhill, New York and Tokyo, 1992)

AUTHOR'S AND PHOTOGRAPHER'S ACKNOWLEDGEMENTS

We would like to thank the following: Ilse Crawford, Ichen Driess, Fiona Dunlop, Anne Furniss,
Japan Airlines, Japan National Tourist Board, Helen Lewis, Eve MacSweeney, Yves Marbrier,
Paola Morretti, Nancee Oku Bright, Hamish and Karen MacAlpine, Andrew Nurnberg,
Simon Withers, Sarah Withers

PHOTO CREDITS

All photographs by Christoph Kicherer except pages: 6 Dana Levy/from Pleasures of the
Japanese Bath published by Perpetua Press; 9 Fototeca Unione Academia Americana; 13
The Ronald Grant Archive; 24-25 Lars Hallen/Design Press; 26 National Trust Photo Library/
Andreas von Einseidel/designed by Sir John Soane; 30 Jordi Sarrá Arau; 31 above Jordi Sarrá
Arau; 31 below © The Estate of Buckminster Fuller. Courtesy Buckminster Fuller Institute,
Santa Barbara; 36 designer Ayse Birsel; 37 Ushida Findlay (UK) Limited/Katsuhisa Kida; 130 far
left Arcaid/Richard Bryant/Architect Seth Stein; 133 far right – 1 Droog Design; 133 far right –
2 Droog Design; 133 far right – 3 Droog Design; 133 far right – 4 Droog Design; 138 above
right Boffi Bagni; 138 centre right Agape; 138 below left Obumex; 139 below left Arcaid/
Richard Bryant/Architect Spencer Fung; 139 above left Boffi Bagni; 139 above right Nito; 139
centre right Agape; 141 below left Boffi Bagni; 141 centre right Katsuhisa Kida/Brookes Stacey
Randall; 142 right Boffi Bagni; 143 left Boffi Bagni; 144 right Droog Design/photographer Hans
van der Mars; 145 left Droog Design; 145 above centre Boffi Bagni; 146 above right Boffi Bagni;
150 Margherita Spiluttini/architect Peter Zumthor; Back Jacket MGM/Courtesy of Kobal

STYLIST CREDITS

Pages: 35 Yves Marbrier; 38-39 Yves Marbrier for Vogue Decoration; 52-53 Fiona Dunlop
for Interni; 64-69 Yves Marbrier for Casa Vogue; 70-71 Yves Marbrier for Vogue (UK);
72-3 Yves Marbrier for Vogue Decoration

*The author, photographer and publishers would also like to thank all the people who allowed
us to photograph their work and in their homes including:*
Marwan Al Sayed, Anderson Architects, Azumaya Inn, BAM Masakazu Bokura, Matt Briffa,
Nancee Oku Bright, Vincenzo De Cotiis, Janet Fink, Valentine and Markus Hansen, Winka
Dubbeldam, Foundation Le Corbusier, Mark Guard, Jim Goldstein, Philip Gumuchdjian, David
Hertz, Philip Johnson, Langlands and Bell, Richard Leplastrier, Philippe Morillon, Jenya Osbourne,
Stuart Parr, John Pawson, Andrée Putman, Charles Rutherfoord, Schindler House, Yvonne
Sporre, Philippe Starck, Ernst Wagner, John Young